MY NAME IS ALMOST

A Memoir

Tia Heard

ISBN: 979-8-9989037-1-7

Printed in the United States of America

Table of Contents

Dedication

To the orphaned children,
The ones I've held in my arms, and the ones I've only held in my heart…
This book is for you.

I am you. You are me.
Every page, every word, every wound stitched into these lines exists because you exist.
Your strength is the reason I began this journey. Your stories echo in mine.
Your pain, your hope, your laughter; I carry it all with me.

May these words wrap around you like a warm embrace.
May you feel seen. May you feel loved.
And may you always know:
You were never forgotten.
You are my why.
You are my heart.

With endless love,

Tia

Dedication continued...

To my parents—
Thank you for giving me a life filled with safety, patience, and unconditional love. To my mother, my biggest cheerleader, who has read every page I've written with more heart than critique. You've championed my words even when the chapters were messy, painful, or unfinished reminding me that my voice matters, even when I doubted it. From the moment you handed me my first journal, you sparked a love for writing that has never left me. This book exists because of you.

To Mr. Curry—
My AP English teacher in high school. You may never read this book or remember who I was among your many students, but I remember *you*. At a time when I was overwhelmed by school and weighed down by the doubt and accusations of the very teachers meant to support me, you did the opposite. You told me I could write. You planted a seed of belief in a teenage girl who didn't yet know how to use her voice; and now, here I am, finally speaking. Thank you for seeing something in me long before I could see it myself.

Introduction
by the Author – Tia Heard

This book was never meant to be written; at least, not by me. For years, I carried these stories in silence, afraid that giving them words would somehow make them too real, too raw, too permanent. But I also knew that silence was slowly eating away at me. There is power in the telling, and this book is my act of reclaiming that power.

"My Name Is Almost" is not just a memoir. It is a mirror. I wrote this for the child I once was— the orphaned girl who didn't know how to scream for help, the teenager who smiled while carrying the weight of trauma, the young woman who kept pushing through life without ever stopping to ask why she was running. But I also wrote this for *you*. For every soul who has felt both invisible and too visible all at once. For the ones who feel like their stories are too messy to be told. For the ones who carry pain in silence. For the ones who have almost given up but haven't. You are not alone. I am you.

This book will walk you through different chapters of my life: my early years in Vietnam, being adopted and raised in America, the challenges of assimilation, the hidden wounds of abuse, the complicated loves that shaped me, and my recent journey back to Vietnam in search of peace and purpose. As you read these pages, you'll travel with me through pain, laughter, trauma, healing, and moments of raw humanity. This is not a story wrapped neatly with a bow. It's messy. It's contradictory. It's real. I've lived with abandonment, abuse, love, loss, and self-sabotage. I've known what it feels like to be lifted by grace and dragged by grief. And I've learned that even in the chaos, even in the uncertainty, our stories matter.

I thank you for holding mine in your hands. And I hope that by the end of it, you'll begin to honor your own. This is my truth, and in reading it, maybe you'll find pieces of yours.

With love,
Tia

Every man has his secret sorrows which the world knows not; and often times we call a man cold when he is only sad." - Henry Wadsworth Longfellow

PHASE 1: Silence
Abandonment, early trauma, isolation

1: Almost

The hum of Ho Chi Minh City wraps around me like a warm, chaotic embrace. Motorbikes zip by in streams of noise and motion, their honks blending into a rhythm that the city seems to breathe to. I'm sitting at a small coffee shop on a bustling street corner, my laptop open, its cursor blinking accusingly at me. It's as if the blank page is challenging me to make the first move.

I grip onto my iced coffee as if I will drink it, but I do nothing. The ice has already begun to melt, swirling into the dark liquid, thinning the taste. My fingers feel numb against the condensation pooling on the plastic cup, but I still don't take a sip.

The waitress comes by again. Her voice is soft, polite, cutting through the background noise. I catch her saying, *"Cô có cần gì không?"* but it barely registers. I nod absentmindedly, hoping it looks like a thank-you instead of dismissal. She lingers for a second, perhaps waiting for me to say something more, but when I don't, she simply offers a polite smile before moving on.

I exhale, staring down at the cup in my hands. The weight in my chest remains. The city moves around me, endless and indifferent, but I am stuck—gripping a coffee I have no intention of drinking, drowning in thoughts I can't quite articulate.

This coffee shop has become my refuge. Over the past month, I've spent hours here, watching the city move through its endless cycles of energy and calm. From the quiet mornings when the streets are still waking up to the electric evenings when they pulse with life, I've sat here, laptop open, and written nothing.

The same question keeps circling in my mind like a storm that won't pass—*why am I even here? What am I doing with my life?* Did starting my own business really make sense, or was it just another impulsive move in a long line of survival-mode decisions? Why am I not fully showing up for it now, when this is what I said I wanted?

I packed up everything and moved halfway across the world to Vietnam, telling myself I needed clarity. Telling myself this would be the space I finally healed. I kept reminding myself that the perk of my job is the freedom to work from anywhere in the world, so why not here, in Vietnam? The very place where everything began for me. If I was going to build something of my own, why not do it surrounded by the roots of my story?

But clarity hasn't come. The noise inside me hasn't quieted. I wake up some days wondering what I've done, other days wondering if I've done enough. Most days, I just sit in the stillness; an unfamiliar kind of quiet that feels more haunting than peaceful.

The truth? I don't know what I'm doing. I don't know where I'm headed. I stare at my laptop like it's supposed to cough up answers, like it's supposed to make sense of all the grief, guilt, chaos, and disorientation that has become my life these past few years. But all it offers is a blinking cursor and the echo of my own thoughts.

The unraveling started long before I came to Vietnam. A slow, steady peeling away of everything I thought made me whole. Friends gone. A dog who was more than a dog. Jobs that didn't last. People I thought would stay but didn't. Identities I clung to, stripped away until all that was left was me—and even then—I wasn't sure who that really was anymore.

Isolation used to terrify me. Now it's just…there. Like background noise I've learned to live with. I've stopped running from it. I let it sit beside me, let it wrap around me like a second skin. Maybe this is what healing really looks like—not the epiphany, not the clarity, but the acceptance of the not-knowing.

**

I came here searching for peace. A softer landing. A version of myself that isn't so weighed down by everything I've been through. But peace is more elusive than I ever imagined. I don't know if it exists in the way I thought it would.

What I do know is this: I'm still here. Still trying. Still waking up and showing up, even if it's messy and inconsistent. And maybe that's the quiet miracle of it all. Not knowing and doing it anyway.

**

Today feels different, though. There's a kind of restlessness in the air, or maybe it's just inside me. My eyes drift to the streets outside, where motorbikes snake through each other like schools of fish in a chaotic sea. The honks, the chatter, the faint buzz of an old fan inside the café—it all melts into white noise.

What do I even write? How do I begin to tell a story that I'm still trying to understand myself? My story doesn't start with a dramatic moment. There's no scene of me clutching a letter from my birth mother, no sudden epiphany about who I am. My story is quieter, stitched together with a thousand small questions: Where do I come from? Who am I supposed to be? What does it mean to belong?

But sitting here, with the city buzzing around me, my mind feels as blank as the page in front of me. I want to start this book—to tell my story—but I don't even know where the beginning is, or if I'm ready to find it.

**

The waitress passes by again, her tray balanced expertly in one hand. She glances at me, and I notice a flicker of concern in her eyes. I must look as lost as I feel. A flicker of movement pulls me from my trance. A stray dog, skinny but with an unmistakable confidence, trots across the coffee shop's tiled floor. Its fur is patchy, its tail wagging half-heartedly as if it's learned not to expect too much kindness from the world. The dog pauses near my table and looks at me, its head tilted to one side, its dark eyes holding a depth I can't quite explain.

The dog lingers, its gaze locked onto mine, studying me just as I am studying it. There's a quiet understanding between us, an unspoken recognition of something familiar…perhaps loneliness, perhaps a shared resilience. Its ribs press against its thin coat, evidence of the hard life it has endured, yet there is still a quiet dignity in the way it carries itself.

I shift slightly in my chair, expecting it to flinch, but it doesn't. Instead, it takes a cautious step closer, sniffing the air as if debating whether I am safe. The café staff pays no mind to the dog's presence; it must be a regular here, wandering in and out as it pleases, looking for scraps or, if it's lucky, a kind hand.

Something about the moment feels significant, like a tiny pause in the chaos of my thoughts. I hesitate, then slowly extend my hand. The dog doesn't move at first, but after a long, quiet moment, it closes the distance and presses its head against my palm. Its fur is rough and wiry beneath my fingers, but the warmth is real. Tangible. A grounding presence amid the whirlwind of uncertainty that has been following me.

For the first time in what feels like hours, I take a deep breath. Maybe I don't need all the answers right now. Maybe, for this moment, just sitting here with this stray dog is enough.

For a moment, the world stills.

**

I blink, brought back to reality. The waitress is still there, waiting patiently. Her lips curve into a small, understanding smile as I finally look up and manage to say, "I'm good, cảm ơn." She nods and moves away, leaving me alone with my thoughts.

The dog lingers next to me, its thin frame casting a faint shadow against the café's floor. Its gaze follows the waitress as she moves behind the counter, watching with an alertness that suggests it has learned to anticipate kindness, or maybe indifference.

It turns to look at me one last time, its dark eyes steady, unreadable. For a moment, I wonder if it sees something in me—something familiar, something lost. Then, without hesitation, it turns and walks toward the front of the café, slipping past the open doorway and vanishing into the endless current of the city.

I watch as it disappears, swallowed up by the pulse of motorbikes and hurried footsteps, its presence fading into the noise of honking horns and distant chatter. And yet, the image of it lingers, stirring something inside me, something small but insistent, like the first spark of a fire.

I exhale slowly, my fingers still hovering over the keyboard. The dog, the moment, the feeling— it all sticks to me, pressing against the part of me that has been questioning everything. Where am I going? What am I doing? Am I just wandering, like that stray, moving from place to place without knowing where I truly belong?

The thought unsettles me. But maybe, just like the dog, it doesn't matter. Maybe moving forward—anywhere, anyhow—is enough.

**

I take a deep breath and focus back on the blank page. Maybe I don't need the perfect introduction. Maybe I just need to start. My fingers hover over the keys, hesitant, before they begin to move. The words come slowly at first, then faster.

My name is Tia, and I don't know where to start, but I think that's okay. Some stories don't begin with certainty; they begin with a coffee shop, a stray dog, and the quiet decision to just start.

I pause, letting the sentence settle on the screen. A faint breeze drifts in from the open door, carrying the scent of motor oil and fried bánh xèo from a street vendor nearby. The noise outside seems softer now, more like a background hum than an overwhelming roar.

I glance around the café. A young couple sits in the corner, laughing over a shared plate of bánh mì. An older man reads a newspaper, his coffee untouched but steaming. The waitress wipes down an empty table, her movements unhurried but precise. Life here is full of small, ordinary moments, yet they feel profound in their simplicity.

I take another sip of my iced coffee, the cold bitterness grounding me. Maybe this is what I need, not answers, but moments. Not a perfect beginning, but a willingness to sit with the questions.

Almost

I came here hoping for inspiration, for clarity. Instead, I'm replaying scenes from a movie I watched years ago: Apocalypto, directed by Mel Gibson. It's not the kind of film you forget. Brutal, raw, and relentless, it's a story about survival against all odds. The main character, Jaguar Paw, is given a nickname by his capturers—"Almost."

Almost.

That name has lingered in my mind ever since, like a stone in my shoe. No matter how many times I shake it out, it finds its way back—settling in, pressing against me, a reminder of everything I've almost been. It's a word that feels too close, too personal. It fits me better than my own name.

Almost should have been mine.

Almost became a lawyer, almost stayed local for college instead of chasing some impossible dream. Almost gotten married to the man I thought I'd spend forever with, almost had children. Almost stayed in each loving relationship instead of pushing them away. Almost got close enough to people to open-up about my deep traumas. Almost wanted to end my life a few times, but somehow, I fought through that. And here I am, in my 30's still not knowing who I really am.

Almost built a life that felt stable.

The word follows me like a shadow, always a step behind, always present. It weaves itself into my story, marking the places where I hesitated, where I turned away, where I let fear or doubt or stubbornness pull me in another direction. It's not just a word, it's a trail of ghosts, a collection of unlived lives, a whisper of what could have been.

Ha…I could write an entirely separate book just cataloging the times I've fucked up in my life. Big mistakes, small mistakes, ones so ridiculous they make me question my own sanity. I've wondered more times than I'd care to admit if there's something wrong with me. Maybe I have some undiagnosed mental disability. Or maybe I'm just wired to self-destruct, to sabotage anything good that comes my way.

**

I pick up my coffee and take a sip, wincing at the bitterness. The waitress glances at me again from across the room, her eyes curious but kind. I wonder what she sees when she looks at me. A foreigner with a laptop and a faraway stare? Or does she sense the storm swirling beneath the surface?

I came to this city looking for something, though I'm not sure what. Peace, maybe. Redemption. A chance to come to terms with the person I've been and the one I want to be. But as I sit here, staring at the blinking cursor on my laptop, all I can feel is the weight of almost.

The search for belonging isn't as simple as it seems. And so here I am, an unmarried woman in my 30s, childless, confused. Seated in a café in Ho Chi Minh, fingers poised over my laptop as I try to put my story into words.

**

I started my own business not too long ago, and the truth is... I have absolutely no idea what I'm doing. It's a venture built more on passion than profit; some might call it foolish, maybe even another misstep in a long line of stupid decisions. I should be focusing on my business, but instead, here I am, sitting in a coffee shop thousands of miles from where I started, trying to write a book I don't even know how to begin. My mind is as blank as the screen in front of me, and I wonder if this is just another thing I'll almost finish.

Sometimes I wonder if this is just another chapter of me stumbling through life. Another attempt at finding myself. I originally wanted to write this—whatever this is—not with the intention of publishing a book, but more as a personal journal, a long, ongoing diary entry—a raw, unfiltered stream of everything I've been through. A way to sift through the noise in my own head, to try and make sense of who I am, where I come from, and where I'm going.

But over the years, people—friends, strangers, therapists—have told me I should write my story. That there's something in it worth sharing. So here I am. Writing. Exposing the raw, sometimes ugly truths of my life in hopes that someone, somewhere, might read this and feel less alone. Maybe they've felt abandoned too. Maybe they've been lost, broken, or unsure of their worth. If they have, and they stumble across my words and find even a sliver of comfort or understanding—then maybe this story matters.

It's not polished. It's messy, it's vulnerable, and it's still being written. Just like me.

**

Outside, the city pulses with life, relentless and unapologetic. Inside, I take a deep breath and place my fingers on the keyboard. This isn't just a book I'm writing—it's a conversation with myself. And for the first time, it feels like I'm finally ready to listen.

The cursor blinks again, but this time, it doesn't feel like a challenge. It feels like an invitation. I start typing, the words flowing like the traffic outside—messy, unpredictable, and alive.

My name is Almost, and this is my story.

2: Scars and Rice Fields

Song Vân

I was born in a rural village called Song Vân. It is a small commune located in the Tân Yên District of Bắc Giang Province in northern Vietnam. It is about a two-hour drive north from Hanoi, Vietnam. Song Vân is a small commune with a population of around 1000 people. Its landscape is typical of the rural regions of Vietnam; the land stretches wide, a patchwork of rice paddies that shift in color with the seasons—lush green in the early months, golden when harvest approaches, then stripped bare as the fields are tilled and prepared for planting once again. The scent of damp soil lingers in the air, mingling with the faint aroma of burning smoke, a familiar rhythm of life that has remained unchanged for generations.

Narrow dirt paths weave through the fields, leading to scattered farmhouses with tin roofs and wooden walls, worn by time and weather. Water buffalo wade through the flooded paddies, their heavy bodies moving with a quiet determination, while farmers—hunched over in their conical hats—plant each seedling with the patience of those who have known no other way of life.

Farming is not just a way to make a living here; it is a lifeline, an unspoken inheritance passed down from one generation to the next. The land provides, but it also demands; early mornings, aching backs, and an understanding that nature is both an ally and a force to be endured. When the monsoons arrive, the rivers swell, threatening to drown the fields that so many rely on. When droughts strike, cracks form in the earth, deep and merciless, a cruel reminder of nature's power.

Beyond the rice fields, small markets appear at dawn, where farmers gather to sell whatever they can—fresh vegetables, livestock, dried fish wrapped in old newspaper. The chatter of buyers and sellers fills the air, a temporary break from the quiet that usually blankets the countryside.

In a place like this, time moves at its own pace. The sun rises, the sun sets, and in between, life is lived in the simplest of ways…without rush, without expectation, but with a resilience that has kept these lands alive for centuries.

**

But Song Vân is not the kind of place people dream about visiting, and it's not the sort of place that would leave an impression on a traveler. It's just an unremarkable dot on the map, a place where life is measured in bowls of rice and long, grueling days under the sun. The roads are dusty, the buildings worn and colorless, the kind of place where time doesn't move forward so much as it circles itself. It's a place where people don't talk about dreams because dreams have no space to grow here. The soil is dry, cracked from years of struggle, and the people wear their exhaustion the way others wear fine silk.

There is nothing to do here. No cafés with soft music playing in the background, no bookstores lined with stories waiting to be discovered. The days are long, monotonous, predictable, the kind that weigh on your chest like a dull, aching pressure. The air always smells of wet earth and smoke, the kind of scent that clings to your skin long after you've left, haunting you with its heaviness. It's the smell of survival, of a place that has forgotten how to hope.

People here don't look for more. They don't search for adventure, for love, for the kind of lives that exist in novels. They wake up, they work, they sleep. Repeat. The cycle is endless, stretching on without a promise of change.

And yet, despite all of that, Song Vân is a place that refuses to disappear. It lingers, stubborn and unyielding, existing not because it is special, but because it simply must.

Poverty

The years preceding and after my birth, poverty wreaked havoc on Song Vân. There was no room for dreams of something better, no time for anything other than the daily grind of survival. People lived in small, dilapidated homes, the kind where everything seemed temporary, as if the walls might collapse at any moment. The ground was uneven and muddy, the streets covered in dust, a constant reminder of the struggle to make ends meet. Life there was hard, and for someone born into the conditions I was, it was even harder.

To many, it was a forgotten place, stuck in the past and ignored by the rest of the country. But for those of us born there, it felt like a trap, as if there were no way out, no future beyond the boundaries of its small, suffocating streets.

The province had a reputation—one that no one spoke about openly, but everyone knew. Bac Giang was notorious for its involvement in drug trafficking and human trafficking, dark industries that lurked in the shadows, destroying lives in ways that no one dared confront. Even now, the province clings to this title as if it's the only defining trait it will ever have, the sole thing that sets it apart from the rest of the world. It isn't a place that welcomes newcomers; it is a place where some people are forgotten, exploited, and left behind.

This is where I was born.

But life, as it often does, took its own course; one that didn't include stability, or even the decency of a soft landing. My mother, still young, naive, and uneducated, seemed to drift through love and responsibility like someone looking for an exit. Pregnancy came easily, but commitment never did. I was an obligation she never asked for, a burden in her eyes long before I took my first breath. The weight of motherhood didn't fit her agenda. So, just weeks after I was born, she left for China, chasing whispers of a better life—something brighter than the poverty and shame that hung over her like a cloud she couldn't shake.

Sometimes I wonder…did she ever look back? Did she pause for even a second to think about the child she left behind? Or had she already made peace with the decision, as if cutting ties would somehow free her from everything she didn't want to be? I ask myself if she ever planned to return, if she carried guilt in her chest the way I carried questions in mine. Or was she so far gone—so wrapped up in trying to outrun her reality—that the thought of me never stood a chance against the life she was chasing?

My father? Who knows. And quite frankly—who cares. He's a shadow, a question mark in the story of my life. Some say he vanished to escape responsibility; others say he was just another casualty of a harsh existence. Either way, he was gone before I made my first breath in this world. To my family, a child like me had no value. I was just another mouth to feed in a town where survival came at a steep price.

A girl like me—just being born female—was already seen as a disadvantage. In the world I came from, where tradition weighs heavy and culture holds tight to old beliefs, being a daughter meant being lesser. I was born into a society where sons are celebrated and daughters are quietly tolerated. The birth of a boy was seen as a triumph, the birth of a girl, a quiet disappointment. Boys were the future; they carried the family name, inherited the land, and were seen as blessings to be proud of. Girls, on the other hand, were often viewed as temporary members of the household, destined to leave and belong to another family through marriage.

In that kind of world, I was born already behind. My worth had to be proven, while boys had theirs handed to them at birth. Love, attention, and even basic opportunities were given sparingly, if at all, to girls like me. I wasn't just unwanted, I was an inconvenient; a reminder of everything a family feared: another mouth to feed, another person to clothe, and someone who, in the eyes of tradition, would never bring value back home.

And so, from the very beginning, I knew that simply existing as a girl came with its own set of invisible scars.

Survival was such a commonality in my hometown. Our neighbor had to breastfeed me because we couldn't afford formula, and there was no mother around to do it herself. It's strange to think about—how even my survival depended on the charity of someone else.

Kin

I wasn't entirely alone in this struggle. I had an older sister, born a few years before me—my first and only constant during a time when everything else felt uncertain. We shared the same mother but had different fathers, and in that, we shared another kind of bond: abandonment. Her father, like mine, had vanished into the fog of poverty and broken promises, leaving behind only his absence. He became a ghost—one never spoken of, never searched for, as if forgetting him was easier than feeling the weight of being left behind. We were both remnants of fractured relationships, two young girls shaped by absence and survival, clinging to each other in a world that often felt indifferent to our existence. We learned to carry the same pain.

Yet even in our closeness, loneliness seeped into the cracks of our relationship. She tried to shield me, to be strong where I was weak, but there was no escaping the cold reality that we were children left to fend for ourselves in a world that seemed indifferent to our existence. We learned to survive by watching, by keeping quiet, by hiding parts of ourselves so we wouldn't be hurt. We learned that vulnerability could be dangerous, that trusting too easily could lead to more pain.

Even now, when I think back to those moments, the weight of almost lingers. My sister and I almost had a family, almost had the security of knowing we were wanted, almost had a future we could believe in.

With no mother or father, my care fell to my mother's family, as tradition dictated. In Vietnam, where family is everything, my grandmother took on the responsibility of raising my sister and I. But in a country where poverty isn't just a condition—it's a life sentence—this was more of a struggle than a blessing.

My sister and I lived with my mother's brother and his wife, sharing a cramped home with their four children—three boys and one girl—as well as my grandmother. With so many people packed under a small hut, life was chaotic. It wasn't just the noise or the lack of space that made it difficult; it was the overwhelming sense that I didn't belong. And it wasn't just a feeling—I knew I wasn't wanted.

My aunt and uncle had no interest in me. If anything, they barely acknowledged my presence, and when they did, it was often with indifference or outright hostility. I wasn't just an outsider in their home; I was an inconvenience. At times, it felt like I was being bullied by my cousins, deliberately excluded from family activities, and left to fend for myself in a house that never truly felt like mine.

**

I don't know why, but when I think back to my time living with my family in Song Vân, it's always the painful memories that surface first. Maybe it's because those moments left deeper marks than I ever understood. The punishments seemed constant, and they were rarely fair. One particular memory haunts me more than any other—so vivid, it feels like it happened yesterday. I was just a toddler, and yet I remember it all: the sharp burn of hot chili peppers used as punishment, forced down my vagina. I screamed. I cried. The pain was unbearable, but even more so was the shame, the confusion, the sense of betrayal.

I've tried to convince myself over the years that maybe I imagined it, that my memory is playing tricks on me. But the details are too clear. The feeling too real. And even if I don't understand why someone would do such a thing to a child, I know it happened. I know it because that day never left me. That day became part of the foundation of how I saw the world: as a place where I wasn't safe, not even in the one place a child should be—at home.

Another vivid memory I have is of the time when the neighbor's dogs attacked me. I had gone to find the neighbor's kids to play with, hoping for companionship, but instead, I was met with an unexpected and terrifying confrontation. The dogs lunged at me, sinking their teeth into my arms and legs. The pain was sharp, and I can still remember the fear and helplessness that followed. To this day, I carry the scars on the back of my legs and arms, reminders of that encounter. I often wonder if that moment further cemented my feelings of being a burden—like I wasn't even worth the protection or care others might offer.

The medical attention I received was far from what any child should endure. My grandmother, with her makeshift medical tools, stitched up my wounds. We couldn't afford proper healthcare, and so, what should have been a simple medical intervention became another act of survival. Maybe that's why my scars are so pronounced, uneven, and rough. Yet, in some strange way, I've come to find beauty in them. They're a mark of survival, a record of a moment that defined me.

What's even stranger is that, despite this painful encounter, I don't fear dogs. In fact, I love them. More than humans, even. Because dogs, unlike people, love unconditionally. They don't ask for explanations. They don't hold grudges. They don't manipulate or shame. They just love—with every ounce of their being.

My love for animals knows no limits. I have a three-legged rescue dog, and I don't see him as broken—if anything—he's proof that you can live a full, joyful life even with missing pieces. He runs, he plays, and he loves without hesitation.

It's ironic, isn't it? How something that should have instilled fear in me only deepened my affection for creatures that, in many ways, have a purer love than most people. You can beat them, neglect them, abandon them, and yet, if you take them back, they'll still greet you with wagging tails, offering unconditional forgiveness. It's funny because, in many ways, I can relate to that.

Run Child

After the dog incident, I tried my best to stay quiet, to be obedient, however, beatings were a frequent part of my life. I never fully understood the reasons behind them. Was it because I misbehaved, or were they simply a release for the frustration and despair caused by our family's poverty? Our house was crowded, filled with my aunt, uncle, sister, cousins, and my grandmother all struggling to survive under the same roof. My aunt, in particular—her anger often boiled over, and her hands became instruments of punishment towards me.

Tradition dictated so many aspects of life, and I often wondered if the beatings were because my presence was a reminder that those traditions had been broken—both my mother and father had abandoned me, leaving a stain on the family's honor. I grew weary of the blows, of the shame and confusion that came with each strike.

I remember the days I grew so tired of it all that I would run. I'd flee into the vastness of the rice fields, letting the tall stalks swallow me up. I became so quick, so practiced at escaping, that eventually, my family stopped chasing me. The rice fields became my refuge, my sanctuary. Out there, with nothing but the wind and the rustling of the plants, I felt a rare sense of safety. It was the only place where I could breathe without fear.

To this day, whenever I see a field of ripe rice or even plants swaying gently in the wind, a wave of peace washes over me. That simple motion, the whisper of leaves brushing against each other, reminds me of the freedom I once found among those fields—a brief escape from a world that felt like it was closing in on me.

I often wonder why my grandmother never stepped in to stop the beatings. Maybe she was simply too consumed with the daily struggle for survival, her energy depleted by the endless demands of poverty. Or perhaps, deep down, she felt the weight of shame too. Maybe she believed that the family's honor had been shattered by my parents' abandonment, and I was a constant reminder of that brokenness. I'd like to believe that my grandmother didn't intervene because she was weighed down by the relentless demands of survival. Truth or not, this thought makes me feel better.

3: A Tin of Cookies

They say I was a quiet child, timid and watchful, with big eyes that seemed to take in everything. I looked different—and in a place like Song Vân, that difference wasn't something to be celebrated. In fact, it was a target. In this rural commune where uniformity brought a sense of belonging, my appearance made me stand out in all the wrong ways. There wasn't curiosity in the stares I received—only suspicion, judgment, and, at times, outright cruelty. I wasn't embraced for being unique; I was resented for it.

Children can be cruel, especially when they mirror the biases of the adults around them. Whether it was my features, my clothes, or simply the way I carried myself, I became an easy mark. Jealousy, misunderstanding, or perhaps just the discomfort of the unfamiliar—all of it came at me like waves.

In Song Vân, where life was already hard, survival often meant blending in. But I couldn't blend in, even when I tried.

"She's the one who got attacked by the neighbor's dog."
"That's the girl with the big eyes."
"The one from the poor family."
"The one with no mom or dad."

These weren't just comments, they were labels. Words whispered behind my back but loud enough to define me. They stuck to me like shadows, following me wherever I went. I wasn't known for who I was, but for what had happened to me, for what I lacked, for how I looked. In a place like Song Vân, where stories spread faster than compassion, these labels became my identity long before I even had the chance to find out who I truly was.

And so, from a young age, I learned what it meant to be an outsider; not in some abstract sense, but in the everyday, gut-wrenching reality of being excluded, ridiculed, and treated like I didn't belong.

I find myself wondering if I was such a bad kid that my family's resentment toward me was justified. Was my mere presence, my existence, a burden to them? Did my physical appearance—so different from the other children—make me an easy target for rejection? It's hard not to think that perhaps I stood out in all the wrong ways. Maybe it wasn't just my behavior, but my difference that made me feel unwelcome. Was I simply too much to bear, or was I simply born into a situation where I never stood a chance?

Three

When I was three years old, I witnessed my first death. It wasn't subtle or abstract, it was a head, cleanly severed in a motorcycle crash, lying on the road like it didn't belong to a human. In my village, no one flinched. No one screamed. It was as if the scene didn't demand a reaction. That's what war does to people…it strips the shock from death. Most of the adults around me were hardened by the Vietnam War; they'd seen worse, so this was just another moment in a long string of brutal memories.

But I hadn't seen worse. I was a child, and I stared at the head on the pavement with wide, confused eyes. No one pulled me away. No one covered my eyes. My family didn't think twice about what it meant for a toddler to witness something like that. And it's moments like this that don't just fade away. They burn themselves into the back of your mind. They become the quiet, lingering proof that even at three years old, I was already being conditioned to survive things no child should ever have to understand.

**

When I was three years old, things in my family didn't improve, they unraveled even more. What was already unstable became even more chaotic, and the fragile sense of safety I was clinging to slipped further away. The beatings became more frequent, and I found myself escaping to the rice fields again and again. Each time, I ran faster, as if my body was conditioned to flee. Perhaps there's irony in how this habit followed me—how I became so adept at running away, even from the good things in my life. I laugh sometimes wondering if I somehow inherited my mother's habit of running away, even though I never truly knew her. Is this the legacy she unknowingly passed down to me—a curse stitched into my DNA, one that I've carried without realizing it?

I laugh, but there's resentment tangled in this laughter. I laugh because logically, I know my mother can't pass down her habits through genetics. And yet, it's as if her choices seeped into my bones anyway. Her leaving—her way of disappearing when things got too heavy—became something I absorbed without realizing. I grew up believing that walking away was normal. That detachment was survival. That leaving was just what people did when life became too much.

I push away what I should hold close.

I hate this part of myself. Maybe that's why I wrote this book—to untangle my own thoughts, to create a self-help guide for my fucked-up thinking. Or maybe I wrote it just to understand myself a little better. I don't know.

**

Anyways, my grandmother, a small woman with a tired face and eyes that held more sorrow than she ever spoke aloud, did her best to keep my sister and I fed, to keep us afloat. Her hands were rough, hardened by years of planting and harvesting rice under a relentless sun, her back bent from endless toil. Despite her strength and her will to survive, love doesn't fill empty bowls, and compassion doesn't soften the harsh realities of life in a developing country.

I didn't fully understand what it meant to be unwanted or forgotten back then, but I felt it. It was in the way neighbors looked at us with pity or avoided us altogether, as if poverty was contagious. It was in the way my grandmother would sigh deeply at the end of each long day, her eyes searching the horizon for answers that never came. I was too young to work, too small to contribute, and so the weight of my existence felt like an additional burden.

Burden

Later that year, the decision for my future was made. I had become too much of a burden for my family. My aunt was the one who ultimately decided that I had to go, and whether my grandmother explicitly agreed or simply went along with it, she did nothing to stop it.

In my mind, sending me to the orphanage wasn't a lack of love; it was an act of survival. She couldn't give me what I needed and keeping me would only mean more suffering for both of us. I was too young to work in the rice fields, too young to understand what was happening. Perhaps she thought the orphanage might give me a chance, however slim, at a better life.

Looking back at my grandmother's decision to give me up for adoption, I wonder if that was her final act of love—a way to offer me an escape from the beatings, from poverty, and to give me the chance to grow up as a child deserves, in a stable, loving home. I'd like to think this was her reason, her gift to me. It's a thought that brings me some comfort, even if I can never truly know for sure.

My older sister remained behind. Even now, I question why they chose me to be given up. She was only two years older than I was—just a child herself. I can't help but wonder if there was something about me, something that made me more disposable. Was I simply unwanted, nothing more?

In those moments, I learned that love could be fierce but fragile, strong but powerless against the unyielding force of poverty. My grandmother did everything she could, but eventually, the only option left was to let me go—to give me up in the hope that I might have a chance at a better life. Even though I was too young to articulate it, deep down, I knew what it meant to be almost— almost part of a family, almost secure, almost loved enough to stay.

The Journey

What stands out the most about that night was how it all happened under the cover of darkness, as if hiding a child's departure would somehow soften the weight of it. I remember the distant hum of the motorbike as a man—someone I didn't recognize—pulled up and lifted me onto the seat behind him. He handed me a tin can filled with cookies, a small offering I didn't understand at the time.

The road stretched endlessly ahead of us, the ride feeling longer than it probably was. The motorbike's engine buzzed beneath me, vibrating through my small frame as we moved steadily forward, the wind stinging my cheeks. The ride felt longer than it probably was; time seemed to lose meaning in that moment. Minutes felt like hours, not because of the distance, but because of the silence. The man driving didn't speak, and I didn't ask. There was a heaviness in the air, thick with things unsaid.

I tilted my head back, letting the wind rush over me, and stared up at the night sky. It was vast and unbroken, the stars scattered like tiny holes punched through black velvet. I traced the constellations with my eyes; shapes I didn't know the names of but somehow felt connected to, as if they had been watching me long before this ride. I kept staring at the stars, expecting them to speak back to me, but they didn't. They just shimmered, distant and indifferent.

On either side, the rice fields blurred into long, dark streaks, their water-logged surfaces catching fragments of moonlight. They looked like mirrors, except there was nothing in them to reflect but the emptiness around me. The fields didn't move or speak, but they bore witness to everything. They had seen many things, I imagined…births, deaths, goodbyes. Now they watched me, silently observing yet offering no comfort.

And so, I sat still, quiet, my arms wrapped tightly around the tin of cookies on my lap, holding onto the only thing I had been given that night. As if, even at that age, I understood life was about being taken, given, forgotten, remembered…without warning and often without explanation.

I was only three years old. What kind of three-year-old thinks this deeply about themselves and the world around them? It feels almost impossible to fathom that such complex thoughts could emerge at such a young age. And yet, the memories of those moments are so vivid, like pieces of a puzzle that I didn't have the capacity to understand at the time.

One day, I had a family. The next, I didn't. There was no gradual unraveling, no slow realization—just a sharp, irreversible break. One moment, I was a child navigating a crowded home, longing for a place where I belonged. The next, I was standing at the gates of an orphanage in Hanoi in the middle of the night, a place I had never seen before but would have to call home. The air smelled different there, thick with unfamiliarity. The voices around me blended into an indistinct hum, their words meaningless as I struggled to make sense of what had just happened. I didn't cry. I didn't ask questions. I simply walked through the doors, knowing there was nowhere else to go.

4: The Cold Place

The metal gate at the Orphanage clanged shut behind me, its echo stretching far into the night, louder in my memory than it probably was in reality. I stood still for a moment, too small to grasp the permanence of what had just happened, yet old enough to feel it in my bones. Someone—a woman—took my hand, guiding me through dim hallways with peeling walls and fluorescent lights that buzzed faintly overhead. The smell of antiseptic and mildew mixed with something else—maybe boiled cabbage or rice left too long in the pot. That smell would follow me for years.

I clutched the tin of cookies tightly. They were dry, crumbly, and stale, but I didn't eat them. I didn't know why, but it felt like the only thing that was mine. I didn't even know the name of the man who gave it to me, but the tin became a strange sort of comfort—proof that someone, at some point that night, had thought I deserved something sweet.

**

The orphanage was a strange, cold place. Its walls seemed to absorb any warmth that tried to enter, leaving behind only the sharp chill of abandonment. It was a world of children like me, all with their own stories of being left behind by parents who couldn't afford or didn't want to stay. We weren't just orphans; we were castaways in a society that had no room for us, trying to find our place in a world that had already forgotten us.

I remember my first night at the orphanage. I arrived late, after most of the other children had gone to sleep. The air was thick with unfamiliar smells: soap, mildew, and something metallic I couldn't place.

They cut my hair short that night. Not gently. There were no warm towels or soft combs. Just scissors and silence. I watched the strands fall to the floor, each snip sounding louder than the last. I remember wondering if I would ever grow it out again.

And then, the shower. Cold. So cold. Water that bit at my skin and made me gasp. Another little girl stood nearby, naked and trembling. She was crying. I wasn't. I don't remember her name, but I remember her face. We'd become close in the weeks to follow—two tiny strangers clinging to each other in a sea of chaos. But that night, we were just two frightened girls, stripped of everything familiar, unsure of what came next.

They gave me a shirt and pants that didn't fit. I remember the waistband sagging and the sleeves swallowing my hands. I remember the bunk bed—top and bottom made of wooden planks. No mattress. Just a woven mat over hard slats. I laid down without a word, staring at the ceiling. Somewhere in the distance, a dog barked.

**

I thought I was just spending the night somewhere else. That's what I told myself over and over again…that this place with strange walls and strangers' voices wasn't forever. I kept waiting. I kept looking at the door, expecting someone from home to walk in and say, "Okay, it's time to go."

Everything around me felt temporary. The bed didn't smell like home. The clothes weren't mine. The voices didn't call me by my name in the way I was used to hearing it. But still, I waited. I thought if I stayed quiet and good, they'd come sooner. Maybe they were just running late.

I didn't understand why no one told me anything. No one said, "You're staying here now." And maybe they didn't need to—because in my head, this couldn't be real. I didn't unpack the few things I came with. I didn't let myself settle in. I kept thinking, "Just one more night," like a countdown I couldn't control.

And even though my family had discarded me—abandoned me without a word—I remained heartbreakingly loyal, like a dog still wagging its tail for the hand that beats it. That was me at three years old.

Despite everything, I waited. I waited for someone, anyone, from my family to walk through that door and take me home. I clung to the hope that they'd come back for me, that it had all been some kind of mistake. I didn't understand how love could be so one-sided, but I felt it all the same—deep, unwavering, and desperate.

And each morning I woke up and saw the same unfamiliar ceiling, the same new faces, I told myself, "Maybe today."

No one came for me.

**

But the days kept passing. One night turned into two. Then three. Then a week. I stopped counting after that.

At first, I still kept checking the door—every creak, every footstep made my heart skip. I thought maybe they got lost. Maybe someone forgot to come get me. I even dreamed about them walking in, calling my name, arms open. But no one ever came.

The other kids started treating me like I belonged there. Not in a warm, welcoming way, but in the way that says, *You're one of us now. This is it.* I began to understand in pieces. Not from words, but from the silence. From the routines. From the fact that no one mentioned my family again.

I remember looking at the tiny plastic bowl I was handed during mealtime. There was a small chip on the side. That bowl started to feel more permanent than anything I had known. That's when I knew this wasn't temporary. This wasn't a sleepover. This was my new life, and no one was coming for me.

**

I wasn't one of the tough kids. I was one of the quiet ones. I blended into the background, a shadow among shadows, trying to make myself invisible. I thought that if no one noticed me, they couldn't hurt me. During the day, I wandered off to other places, much like I had fled into the rice fields. I ran—not physically this time—but emotionally. The silent thoughts were my escape, just as the fields had been a place where I could leave everything behind and disappear, if only for a while. Running, whether in my mind or physically, became second nature to me. It was the one thing I could rely on, a reflex that gave me a way to escape, to keep moving when everything else felt out of control. Running was what I knew best.

The days were a fight for survival, but not in the way people imagine. It wasn't just about having enough food or a place to sleep, though those were constant concerns. It was a fight for love, for the smallest scraps of affection that could make you feel human. A pat on the head from a caretaker, a kind word from a visitor; these moments were rare and fleeting, but they meant everything. They were proof that you were seen, that you mattered, even for just a second.

The competition for attention was fierce. Every child wanted to be the one the caregivers liked best, the one visitors might take a special interest in. It wasn't a conscious effort, but we all felt it—the unspoken battle to be noticed, to be chosen, to feel wanted. For some, this meant acting out, creating chaos to draw eyes their way. For others, it meant being the "good" child, obedient and helpful, hoping that compliance would earn affection. I didn't know how to fit in either way. I just stayed quiet, hoping that someday, someone would see me anyway.

But the truth was, being quiet often made you invisible. It meant you were the last one to get a second helping of food, the one overlooked when new clothes were handed out, the one no one picked during playtime. I remember when a visitor would bring candy or treats, they never lasted long in my hands. Another child would quickly snatch them away and run off. I almost had the nerve to fight back, but I didn't. I just let it happen.

Many days, I would watch the other children interact, their bonds growing quickly as they found solace in each other's company. But for me, it was different. I didn't know how to connect with them. I closed myself off from the world and I wasn't sure how to open it again. I was afraid of letting anyone close, afraid of being hurt, of being left behind again. So, I kept my distance.

**

There were a few children who arrived at the orphanage in pairs or small groups—siblings clinging tightly to one another. I remember watching them with a quiet, aching envy. They had something I didn't: someone who knew their story, someone who shared their past. Even in such a strange and unfamiliar place, they had each other to hold onto, to whisper to at night, to cry with when things got too hard.

I longed for that kind of connection. I imagined what it would feel like to have a sibling beside me, someone who could say, *"We'll be okay."* But I had no one. I was alone in every sense of the word. And though I tried to be strong, deep down, I envied their bond. Because no matter how hard things got, at least they weren't going through it alone.

Trust

Trust was a luxury we couldn't afford. Trust was something that I had a hard time with, especially in a place like the orphanage, where children like me were abandoned, left to fend for ourselves without the comfort of familiar faces or a sense of security. I didn't know how to trust, how to open up, and for a long time, I kept my guard up. The pain of abandonment ran deep, and I carried it with me in the silence of the orphanage, where trust was rare and friendship felt like an impossible luxury.

Despite this, I grew close to another girl. She was the girl who was with me the first night I came to the orphanage; the one who cried all night. While I stood frozen in silence, she wept openly, her sobs filling the sterile room. In that moment, even though we hadn't yet spoken, I felt connected to her. Her pain was loud, mine was quiet, but they came from the same place. We had a bond that, at the time, felt as close to family as I had ever known. We danced and played together when we could, the only moments when I felt a fleeting sense of joy. But outside of this friendship, I had no one. Friendship wasn't easy in a place where everyone was fighting their own battles.

The orphanage was a place that tested you, broke you down, and forced you to rebuild yourself with whatever scraps of strength you could find. It taught me that love wasn't guaranteed, that it was something you had to fight for, even if you didn't know how. It showed me how much I wanted to be seen, to be chosen, to belong. Some nights, I would lie awake, staring at the ceiling, trying to make sense of it all. Why wasn't I enough for people to want me? What was wrong with me that made me so easy to leave behind? I remember wondering what I'd done wrong. Was I too quiet? Too timid? Did my big eyes make people uncomfortable? I didn't understand that none of it was my fault, that I was simply born into a world where love alone wasn't enough to overcome the weight of poverty and tradition.

**

It's odd, but in some ways, an orphanage feels a lot like a jail. It's a place where time drags on, where some people emerge stronger, while others, like myself, carry a lot of unresolved anger and resentment. While I don't blame the orphanage or the caretakers for my mental state, I can't deny the fact that the isolation there gave me all the time in the world to think—too much time.

Back in my hometown of Song Vân, the harsh realities of poverty and survival didn't leave room for reflection. Life was about just getting by, about the constant hustle. But in the orphanage, the stillness allowed my thoughts to fester and grow darker. It was there that I began to feel the weight of my own thoughts—the confusion, the resentment, the sense of abandonment—and these feelings, over time, became a part of who I am. In a strange way, I think the orphanage shaped the person I would become, for better or worse. I wonder sometimes if the fucked up struggles I face now can be traced back to the lonely hours spent there, trapped with my thoughts and emotions.

**

The nights were always my favorite though. Still are. There's something about the stillness of the world after dark that brings me peace. Even now, I get most of my work done while everyone else sleeps. Maybe it's because nighttime always felt like mine—quiet, undisturbed, away from the chaos of the day.

Back then, in the orphanage, those hours were when I came alive in my own little world. Since proper education wasn't really accessible to us, I started teaching myself. I would lie awake, playing imaginary games—counting as high as I could, teaching myself numbers, inventing challenges in my mind. Once, I had seen old men in Hanoi sitting on the sidewalk playing chess. I stood there silently, watching every move like it was a secret code being revealed. Later, back in my room, I would try to recreate their moves in my imagination.

It might sound strange, but I made up my own versions of checkers and chess—played entirely in my head—night after night. Years later, when I watched *The Queen's Gambit*, I was stunned. A young girl, orphaned, playing chess at night while the world slept. It felt surreal. Familiar. Like someone had reached into my past and pulled it onto the screen.

These are the moments that remind me why I'm writing this book. Because somewhere out there, another person might read these words and feel seen. Understood. And if even one person feels that connection, then I've done my job as a writer.

**

Despite the limited resources, the orphanage tried to provide us with experiences, to show us that the world was bigger than the walls we lived within. They took us on trips, like to the beach, in an attempt to offer us some sense of normalcy and joy. But the memories I hold are not of those trips. The moments that stand out to me are filled with discomfort, pain, and loneliness. Perhaps, deep down, I couldn't understand how to let myself feel the joy others might have. I was such a shy child, always withdrawn, always hiding from fun and connection. I couldn't even manage to smile; every photo taken of me at the orphanage is a portrait of a frown, of fear.

What I remember most is the way the orphanage handled our day-to-day needs. Every night, the caretakers would line us up for lice treatments, meticulously combing through our hair. It was a small, yet constant reminder of how little we had, how different we were from other children. I was malnourished, my body showing the signs of an unwanted child.

We only wore our nicest clothes on rare occasions—usually when visitors were scheduled to tour the orphanage, or during special events like photo sessions meant for potential adoptive families. Those moments felt staged, a temporary pause in our reality so we could be presented as neat, smiling versions of ourselves; children worthy of a second chance.

There is a part of me that wonders if I missed out on the good days, or if there really weren't any. Maybe I never learned how to be happy in that environment because, from such a young age, I was familiar with rejection, with the deep sense of abandonment. I don't know.

I wonder if, perhaps, my inability to smile was more than just shyness. Was it a deep, unspoken awareness that I wasn't wanted, that I was just one of many? I don't have the answers. I wish I did. All I know is that those days shaped me in ways I'm still learning to understand.

5: Echoes in the Alley

While the orphanage was organized and controlled for the most part, there were moments when children aged five and older were allowed a little more freedom. It wasn't often, but sometimes we were given brief windows where we could venture off on our own. I remember one of those days.

It was just another morning, and I was on my way to class. Orphans like me were kept in separate classes from the local children, which made us feel even more apart from the rest of the world. It was a short walk, but to me, it felt significant. As I made my way through the streets, I was caught in the whirlwind of Hanoi's busy streets. The constant hum of motorbikes filled the air, weaving in and out of the traffic.

Hanoi, back then, was as vibrant as it is today, but the streets felt even more alive with the noise and motion. The motorbikes seemed to outnumber the cars, and the bustle of the market filled every corner. As I walked, I paid little attention to the chaos around me. All I could think about was getting to class. It was a small goal in the sea of daily responsibilities. Yet, that walk, that moment of autonomy, was one of the few times I felt a small sliver of control in a life otherwise shaped by rules and limitations.

I was starting to get familiar with the streets, the rhythm of the city, and the winding alleyways that threaded through Hanoi. One particular alleyway stood out to me—it was narrow, quiet, and tucked away from the main roads. I gravitated toward it by instinct, always finding comfort in its closeness and the solitude it offered. These small, confined paths had become a part of me over the years, a reflection of the space I grew up in. In Song Vân, everything felt tight and restrictive—physically, emotionally. No matter how hard I tried, my feet seemed to guide me down these familiar alleys, almost as if I were searching for something I couldn't name.

It wasn't necessarily a choice; it was a habit. There were no rice fields to escape to. Just small alleyways. These alleyways had always been a source of comfort for me, offering a sense of safety in a world that often felt overwhelming and unfamiliar. They were my refuge, the place where I could retreat, away from the chaos and noise of the streets, where I felt like I could breathe, even if just for a moment.

**

But that day was different. The narrow passageways, once a sanctuary, suddenly felt oppressive, closing in on me rather than offering any form of solace.

Something had shifted in the air that day, something I couldn't quite grasp, but it made my usual path feel more like a trap than a safe haven. The walls seemed too close, the shadows too dark, and the bustling sounds of Hanoi, once comforting in their constant hum, now felt like a constant reminder that I was just a small, unnoticed child in a city that barely seemed to care. It was as if the world had turned its back on me, and these once-familiar alleyways, which had been my shelter, now only amplified the sense of loneliness that had crept in, threatening to swallow me whole.

As I continued down the alleyway, I noticed a group of boys, perhaps four or five years older than me, following closely behind. At first, I thought nothing of it. They looked like they were heading to class, just like me. But soon, their quiet whispers and smiles began to feel unsettling. I couldn't figure out why they were smiling—maybe I had something on my clothes? Maybe they were just making fun of me? Whatever the reason, I tried to ignore them and kept walking, hoping they would lose interest.

But as I walked further, I felt an unexpected grip on my backpack, followed by hands on my arms and legs. The world around me seemed to blur, everything happened so fast that I couldn't process it all. I did not have time to scream, let alone comprehend it all. It felt like I was in a nightmare, my mind racing, but my body frozen. There was no time to scream, no time to escape. The panic surged through me, but the only thing I could do was continue to move, hoping I could break free.

I didn't understand what was happening until the terror set in. One of the boys held me down, his face a blur, his grip unrelenting on my mouth.

I blacked out several times as the suffocating grip of hands pressed against my mouth and nose. My eyes were open, yet I couldn't breathe. I couldn't scream, couldn't even find my voice. Despite the overwhelming pressure, I fought. I kicked and struggled with all the strength I had, propelled by something deeper within me. It wasn't just the immediate threat of those boys—it was the rage from all the pain I had experienced in my young life, the anger from all the rejection, neglect, and suffering I had already endured.

At just five years old, I felt so much—so much hatred for the world that had treated me so cruelly. I wanted to escape, to leave it all behind, but some part of me refused to give up. My body fought to stay alive, to stay in this world, even when everything in me longed to escape it. It was as if my mind and body were locked in a battle—my soul desperate to let go, but my consciousness unwilling to abandon the fight.

The boys continued to laugh, their voices mingling with my silent screams. One of them grabbed something nearby—a long, jagged stick—and I remember the terror in that moment when it was aimed between my legs. I was too young to fully grasp what was happening, but my body knew. I felt the violation even before pain took over. It wasn't just the physical agony—it was the complete loss of control, the shattering of whatever innocence I had left. I remember the way my body froze, how the world blurred around me, and how something in me began to break, quietly and invisibly. It's hard to explain that kind of horror, but it imprints itself deep, in ways I'm still trying to understand today.

**

No one came to rescue me that day. It was just another instance in my life where rejection and abandonment felt like an unspoken rule, an inevitability I had grown accustomed to. But at the time, I didn't think about it in those terms. All I could think about was why no one was coming to help me. Why was I alone in this moment of terror? My life, up to that point, had seemed to be a series of unfortunate events—this was simply another one to add to the list.

I don't know how my five-year-old self managed to hold it together in the midst of such chaos, but somehow, my survival instincts kicked in. My small body, driven by a primal need to escape, fought with every ounce of energy I had left. There was a fire deep within me that refused to let go, even when every other part of me wanted to. In that moment, it wasn't about thinking, it was about fighting to stay alive. And despite the overwhelming odds stacked against me, despite the feeling of being completely powerless, I fought back with a ferocity I didn't know I had.

I fought with everything I had, flailing, kicking, desperate to get away. Every time I kicked, trying desperately to get away, the stick was forced deeper in my vagina. The ground beneath me turned red, stained with blood. My legs were slick with it. But somehow, I couldn't feel the pain—at least not in the way I expected. My body went numb, but my mind didn't stop. I kept fighting. Something in me refused to give up, even as everything around me felt like it was shattering.

**

I kept fighting. I kept shifting my body, pushing against the hands that restrained me, moving as much as I could, until suddenly, something shifted. More hell came next. A sharp stab under my chin. The metallic taste of blood filled my mouth. More pain followed when one of the boys took a lit cigarette and pressed it against my skin. The heat seared into me, but I couldn't scream.

I couldn't breathe. I felt my body freeze, not in defense but in surrender. At that moment, all my strength, all my will to fight, faded away. I stopped struggling. Strangely, though, I never felt any pain—not then, not during the ordeal, and not in the immediate aftermath. Even now, I can't explain why. Perhaps my body had gone into survival mode, numbing me to the agony, or maybe my mind had already begun to shield me from the weight of what had happened.

I was no longer fighting to escape; I was just waiting, waiting for it to end, for the torture to stop. I wanted peace. I wanted to disappear. The agony of it all drowned out any hope of survival, and for a fleeting moment, I longed for my life to be over—anything to stop the torment. But it continued. Hot agony seared my skin where they pressed lit cigarettes against me. The smell of burning flesh fused my nostrils.

This is when I played dead. I stopped fighting, closed my eyes, and simply let whatever would happen next unfold. It's strange to think about now—the survival instincts that kick in, even in a child so young. My five-year-old self instinctively shifted into survival mode, something I never thought I would experience. For the rest of that time, I remained still, quiet, and stopped resisting. Whether they grew bored with me or truly believed I was dead, I'll never know. But eventually, they lost interest and walked away, leaving me alone in the alley.

I was broken, bruised, and burned, but somehow, I was still alive. While most would expect a child to scream for help, I didn't. All I wanted in that moment was to protect myself, to retreat inward, to make everything disappear. I wasn't thinking about justice or rescue—I was thinking about how to hide. I wanted to wash away the blood, cover the bruises, and return to some version of normalcy, as if I could rewind time back to that same morning before everything changed.

**

I didn't cry. I stood up slowly, shakily, and all I could think about was not the pain or what had just happened—but whether I'd be punished when I returned to the orphanage. That fear gripped me more than anything else. My five-year-old mind didn't have the language or the understanding for what had just occurred. I just knew I had to clean up fast. Because in my world, punishment was inevitable. That's how life had been—one beating after another, so much so that even a violent attack like this didn't seem like the worst part of my day.

It's fucked up, even now, to look back and realize that I wasn't afraid of the boys or the violence—I was afraid of the consequences of simply existing with those wounds. My mind had been conditioned in such a twisted way that survival meant silence. The thought of the caretakers finding out terrified me more than anything else. I didn't want to imagine what they'd say, what they'd do. I had seen enough punishments to know that pain was always waiting, especially for those who caused trouble or brought shame. So, I decided to stay quiet, like I always had.

That's what trauma does—it rewires you. And at just five years old, I had already learned to silence my pain, to hide my truth, and to keep walking as though nothing had happened. What could I possibly clean up? What could I even begin to hide? The blood, the bruises, the shame— it all felt impossible to cover.

But still, I tried. The cigarette burns on my back, upper arms, and chest could be hidden from the world. These were the kinds of scars that could easily be covered by my school uniform, tucked away from public view. I straightened my shirt, tucked it neatly under my skirt, and adjusted my socks like I was getting ready for another ordinary day. I spat into my hands and used the moisture to scrub the blood from my legs, now drying and crusted against my skin. I kept spitting—over and over—desperate to feel clean, desperate to erase the shame clinging to me.

I didn't have water. I didn't have soap. All I had was spit and panic, so I used what I had. I rubbed harder, trying to wash away the filth, trying to make myself whole again. Finally, when the blood on my legs were gone, I slipped my shoes back on as if nothing had happened. As if I could pretend my body wasn't still trembling. One task done.

But now, the blood trailing from my chin was another problem—a visible truth I couldn't easily hide. I had to figure out what to do with it… and quickly.

I clutched my chin tightly with my right hand, feeling the warm, sticky blood seep through my fingers. Each step felt like a challenge as I struggled to keep the blood from dripping onto the pavement. I had to make it stop—the blood, the dripping, the evidence. I pressed my hand beneath my chin, panicking not because of the pain—but again—because of what might come next. My fear wasn't rooted in the rape itself; it was what awaited me back at the orphanage.

I ripped a piece of fabric from my shirt, dabbing it hastily around the stab wound under my chin, hoping it would stop bleeding. I can still recall the metallic taste of blood as it trickled into my mouth, thick and unrelenting. I swallowed it instinctively, too shocked to spit it out, too focused on the act of moving forward. When the bleeding beneath my chin finally slowed, a strange feeling came about—pride. Not the kind that comes from achievement, but a warped sense of relief.

**

I had cleaned myself up well enough to avoid further punishment. In my five-year-old mind, that meant success. That meant safety. It's disturbing to realize that at such a young age, I had already internalized a world where hiding pain was a survival skill, and avoiding beatings felt like a win. That was the twisted reality I lived in. I was proud that I could hide my scars so well.

Yet, they have stayed with me—etched into my skin as a permanent reminder of that day. To this day, I can still see the faint scrapes and burns on my body, the marks I earned as I tried desperately to slide away on the rough concrete. The stab wound under my chin looks like a lightning rod, a sick, dark form of art. It's unsettling to think about, the disconnect between the visible wounds and the absence of physical sensation. The blood, the struggle, the fear—they were all real. But the pain? It never registered, as though my body refused to acknowledge it.

Even today, when I revisit that moment, the physical sensations elude me, replaced instead by an overwhelming fog of confusion and disbelief.

Small Lies

When I returned to the orphanage, I lied. I said I'd fallen hard while riding a bike with some of the kids. The words came so naturally, like they'd been waiting on my tongue for days, and no one questioned them. Not the caretakers, not the other children, not even the nurse who meticulously cleaned and stitched the wound under my chin. I dared not show anyone the cigarette burns that laid beneath my clothes. Luckily, the injuries were still too fresh—there hadn't been enough time for the bruises to fully surface yet, so no one asked for more details. I was relieved. How could I explain what had really happened when I didn't even understand it myself?

That night, I laid with my eyes wide open, staring into the dark. My body ached, but the pain inside was sharper. I didn't cry. I didn't speak. I just existed in that quiet, hollow space, unable to process what had been taken from me, unable to find the words to name it.

I was only five years old, caught in a storm of emotions I couldn't name. Fear, confusion, and a numbness that seemed to weigh down my small body clouded my mind. The pain on the surface was almost easier to handle than the turmoil inside. It was simpler to focus on the sting of alcohol on raw skin or the tight pull of stitches than to face the truth.

What was the truth, anyway? I couldn't wrap my head around it. There was a void where clarity should have been, a hollow ache I couldn't describe. The adults around me saw only the visible injuries and accepted the neat story I'd fed them. But inside, I was unraveling, trying to make sense of the chaos in my life with the limited understanding of a child.

As the days passed, I began to internalize the lie, burying the memory of what really happened deeper within me. It was safer that way. Safer to live in the narrative I created than to confront the darker reality lurking beneath it.

6: The Bread We Shared

Dissociation became my refuge at the age of five, though I didn't know it at the time. It was as if my mind couldn't take any more of the twisted thoughts, so it began to dissociate, shutting itself off from the horror around me. It was as if my mind instinctively built a wall to separate me from the things I couldn't understand or bear to face. I didn't want to talk about what happened—not because I was keeping a deliberate secret, but because I simply didn't have the tools to articulate it. I couldn't name the emotions or make sense of the experience, so I pretended it never existed.

Each time the memory tried to surface, I pushed it down, locking it away in a part of myself I didn't dare explore. It was easier to live as though nothing had happened, to carry on with the story I'd told about falling off my bike. In my young mind, denial felt like safety. It was a way to keep the fear, confusion, and pain at arm's length, a survival mechanism that became second nature.

This detachment seeped into other parts of my life. It wasn't just about ignoring what had happened, it was about disconnecting from feelings altogether. The fog I lived in was both a shield and a burden, making the world feel distant and unreal. I didn't understand why I couldn't just be like other kids, carefree and present. Instead, I floated through my days as if watching someone else's life unfold.

I became numb, distant, as if I were no longer truly living. I started moving through life like a robot, following what was expected of me, but without any real feeling behind it. At this point, I had lost my only friend at the orphanage to adoption, and I was left to face everything on my own. My thoughts became my only company, and I began to learn how to hide everything I was feeling. I learned to bottle up my emotions, to shut up when it mattered, and to keep quiet to avoid hurting anyone or getting into trouble. I hid my true self, slipping deeper into silence and becoming more reserved with each passing day. The words I never spoke, the truths I buried, became the shield I used to survive.

Over time, the act of pretending became indistinguishable from reality. I buried the truth so deeply that even I struggled to find it. But the cost of that escape was steep. The numbness I relied on to protect myself also left me isolated, unable to truly connect with others or with my own emotions. It was a silence I carried for years, one that shaped how I saw the world—and myself.

That incident stripped away the last remnants of my innocence. I stopped believing in many things. I became cold, a hardness settling inside me like stone. Anger brewed beneath the surface, and I didn't know where to put it. I was only five years old.

**

Even writing about this event fills me with so much anger toward society for failing me. I can't help but question if it's selfish of me to feel this way, to resent the very systems that were supposed to protect me yet left me to fend for myself. A child enduring such trauma alone—it's bound to distort someone. I think about who I might have become if this hadn't happened to me, and the thought lingers, unsettling and haunting. Would I have been different, able to trust and feel more at peace, instead of carrying these scars? What if someone, anyone, had stepped in when I needed it most? The "what ifs" will always linger.

**

What a time to be alive, in all its chaos and confusion. That year shaped so much of who I became, in ways I still don't fully understand. My mindset, already fractured by the years before, only became more complicated, more tangled in itself. The events that unfolded around me didn't help—if anything, they made it worse. It was as though I was trapped in a spiral, one that seemed to tighten with every passing day. The more I tried to make peace with everything, the more disordered my thoughts became. In hindsight, that year marked the beginning of a deeper internal struggle.

I developed a deep well of hatred and anger toward everyone around me. But I couldn't pinpoint who I was truly angry at—was it my family? Society? The boys who raped me? Myself? Back then, I didn't have the words or the understanding to express what I was feeling. So, I kept it all locked inside. Silence became my companion, my way of coping, my method of survival. It was easier that way, hiding everything from the world and from myself.

At the age of five, I desperately needed guidance and love. I desperately needed therapy. The loneliness felt suffocating, and I accepted it as the harsh reality of life. I wish I could go back and tell my five-year-old self that this pain wouldn't last forever. I wish I could kneel to give that child a comforting hug, whispering that things would one day change. There are so many things I wish I could say—to reassure, to soothe, to offer hope. But back then, I didn't know how to believe in anything beyond the struggle.

All I know is, my mind was forever changed that day. It distorted my thinking, rewiring the way I processed everything around me. The world was no longer a place of possibilities; it was a battleground where survival meant expecting the worst. I hated everything and everyone. Hate—such a simple emotion, so easy to feel. It's a word that flows effortlessly onto this page, like it's a natural response to the weight of the world. It's a feeling that comes without effort, like an instinct, so easy to give in to.

**

I glance down at my coffee—now diluted and watery. With a slight wave of my hand, I catch the attention of the waiter and order another iced coffee, hoping maybe a fresh cup will settle something in me. I stand up, stretching my legs, trying to release the tension coiled in my body.

It's almost laughable, really…this scene. Me, sitting in a cozy café in Ho Chi Minh City, surrounded by chatter, the hum of conversation, the clinking of cups. And yet, none of these people around me would ever guess what's boiling beneath the surface. I smile politely, just like I've done all my life. I've mastered the art of hiding everything—my pain, my fury, my chaos—beneath a calm, composed shell to the public.

I catch myself wondering: what would happen if I stood up and told everyone here how angry I really am? If I spoke my truth, unfiltered and raw—would they understand? Would they look at me with compassion or pity? Or would they shrink back, uncomfortable, unsure, silently judging? Would they whisper that I'm unstable, maybe even think I belong in a hospital somewhere?

But the truth is, I'll never know. Maybe it's better that way. Maybe it's safer that they don't see. Just like it's always been.

**

I look at my laptop screen, its glow reflecting the chaos within me. The pages are full—paragraph after paragraph of memories, thoughts, truths I've spent so many years burying. The words are raw and honest. Still, the anger lingers. It coils in my chest like smoke, heavy and unresolved. No matter how much I write, it doesn't disappear. My fingers hover over the keyboard, but I know I need to step away. Just for a moment.

I close the laptop slowly, almost like I'm closing a door on something that's screaming to stay open. The café is buzzing around me—soft conversations, clicking keys, laughter from across the room—but I feel like I'm underwater, muted and disconnected. I rise from my seat, take a sip of my newly arrived coffee, and step outside into the heat of Ho Chi Minh City.

The air hits me instantly. Humid, thick, and alive with noise. Motorbikes zip past in a blur, street vendors call out their offerings, and the scent of grilled food floats in the air. Life is pulsing around me, and for a moment, I let it carry me. I stand at the edge of the street, watching it all move. I'm not ready to go back inside yet. My heart is still pounding too loudly.

I find a shaded spot near a flower cart and lean against the building, closing my eyes. I try to breathe through the ache in my chest. I tell myself I'm okay, that I'm safe now, but the child in me isn't convinced. She's still waiting for something to go wrong. I feel her, angry and tired, and I know she's still fighting.

Maybe that's why I'm writing this. Not just for healing—but to make space for her. To let her be seen. To remind myself that stepping outside, even for a breath, is part of the process too.

Break Bread

My eyes instinctively drift across the street. There, trotting aimlessly along the edge of the sidewalk, is the same scruffy dog I saw earlier in morning. Something about his slow, cautious movements mirrors the ache I carry in my chest. We lock eyes for a brief moment; something between recognition and curiosity passing between us. Without thinking, I search for the nearest food vendor and buy a small loaf of bread.

I cross the street carefully, holding the bread like it's something sacred. As I approach, the dog stiffens, alert but not aggressive. I crouch down slowly and tear the bread in half, placing a piece on the ground in front of him. He sniffs it cautiously, then looks up at me again before finally taking a tentative bite. His tail flicks once, and that's enough for me to sit down right beside him, knees pulled to my chest, the rest of the bread resting in my hand.

We sit there in quiet companionship, sharing a meal like old friends who don't need words to understand one another. I break off a bite and chew slowly, then offer him another piece. He accepts it, this time with less hesitation. The sidewalk is hard beneath me, and passersby glance at me like I'm a little strange—this woman without a chair—sitting on the curb, feeding bread to a street dog like it's the most natural thing in the world.

And maybe, for me, it is. There's something grounding in this moment, something pure in the exchange. We're both a little lost, a little rough around the edges, but here we are…eating cheap bread and existing together in a city that keeps moving. I know I must look ridiculous, but I don't care. For now, I am simply grateful to be understood, even if only by a dog who knows what it's like to survive without needing to explain why.

**

The dog settles beside me, and for the first time all day, I feel something loosen in my chest—a weight lifting, just slightly. The traffic blurs past us, motorbikes zipping by with a hum, horns echoing in the distance, but I don't flinch. The chaos of the city fades behind the quiet moment I'm sharing with this stray soul. He nudges closer with his shoulder touching mine. There's a comfort in his closeness, in his simple presence. Neither of us asks anything of the other, yet we both seem to understand this pause is necessary.

I glance down at the last chunk of bread and break it in two again. One half for him. One half for me. He chews noisily but content, and I follow suit, chewing slowly as if the act itself might digest some of my anger. It's strange, how feeding him feeds something in me too—a tiny spark of softness I didn't think I had left today. I wonder where he sleeps at night, whether he's ever belonged to someone, or if he's always wandered like this, looking for scraps of comfort in a world that often turns cold.

There's something about him—worn but resilient—that reflects back pieces of myself I've tried to ignore. We're both survivors in our own way. Maybe that's why he didn't bark or run, why I didn't hesitate to sit beside him. There's no judgment between us. Just two beings who've known what it's like to go unnoticed, to be hurt, to be left behind—and yet, we're still here. Breathing. Eating. Sharing bread like it's communion.

The heat rises off the pavement, the sweat clings to my back, and yet I remain there, grounded. Maybe I needed this moment more than I knew. Not a therapist's office. Not another chapter in my book. Just this—me and a dog who doesn't need me to explain why I'm angry, why I'm sad, or why I'm tired. He just sits, licking crumbs off the sidewalk, his tail wagging gently as if to say, "You're okay. You made it through today." And for now, that's enough.

**

In truth—

There have been countless moments in this day where I've had to pause while writing; halted by waves of anger and resentment. I once believed that pouring these words onto paper would bring me closer to peace. But now, I sometimes question whether revisiting such raw memories is helping or hurting. Still, I keep writing. Because deep down, I know there's someone out there who feels the same heaviness in their chest, someone screaming silently for their story to be heard. Maybe they don't have the words yet, but maybe my words can help carry theirs. That thought alone reminds me that this pain has a purpose.

**

I glance at the dog one more time. The bread we shared is now gone, every last crumb, and I realize I don't even know how long we've been sitting together on this sidewalk. Time has folded in on itself during this moment of quiet companionship. For just a while, the world felt still. But reality calls—I remember my laptop still inside the cafe, unattended. I trust the staff; they've grown familiar with me over the past month. Still, something tugs at me to return, just in case.

I slowly rise to my feet and brush the dust from my pants. The dog looks up at me, ears twitching slightly. His eyes meet mine, and though he can't say a word, I understand him completely. There's contentment in his gaze. A silent thank you. A knowing. And in that simple look, something inside me settles. His happiness brings me a strange sense of peace, like he's gifted me something just by being here.

I offer a soft smile, the kind that feels new on my face today, and give him a final nod before turning toward the cafe. The air feels lighter as I walk back in. My steps, though slow, carry more ease than they did earlier. The heaviness in my chest hasn't disappeared, but it's loosened its grip.

**

Inside, the familiar hum of coffee machines and quiet chatter greets me. My laptop is exactly where I left it, untouched. I slide back into my seat, heart steadier than before. Outside, the dog lies down in the sun, belly full, tail still. And somehow, in the middle of this city, in a country that once held so much pain for me, a stray dog has reminded me that even small, quiet connections can bring clarity.

7: The Protection We Don't See

I've never considered myself deeply religious, but I can't help but wonder about the countless times I've been in danger, only to somehow make it out alive. If I could count the number of those close calls and had a dollar for each one, I would be richer than I ever expected.

I've traveled to places most tourists would never dream of. Small, isolated villages where the roads are barely paved, the streetlights don't exist, and the only people who pass through are locals who've lived there their entire lives. I've been the only foreigner in entire districts. No tour buses, no guided maps, no luxury resorts. Just raw, real, rural life.

I've been on motorbikes driven by strangers down pitch-black roads, with no GPS, no phone signal, and no idea if I'd even make it to a bed that night. I've slept in jungle huts, boarded buses with bars on the windows, and wandered into towns so remote that even locals questioned what I was doing there. I've eaten food I didn't recognize, in places where no one spoke a word of English—and yet— I always made it out. Sometimes barely.

I've been in situations that weren't just uncomfortable—they were dangerous. Men twice my size approaching me in alleyways out to rob what was in my backpack. Border crossings where passports were confiscated. Getting caught in violent weather with no shelter for miles. Losing transportation options in unfamiliar terrain. If anything had gone wrong, I might not be here to write this.

I've found myself in situations that, in hindsight, sound almost unbelievable; moments that straddled the line between recklessness and sheer survival. There was a time I got into a taxi in a remote rural town, only to find out too late that the driver wasn't just a driver—he was one of the area's most notorious drug dealers. Somewhere along an isolated stretch of road, surrounded by rice fields and without a single bar of cell service, he stopped the car, turned around, and demanded ten times the fare. His threat was clear: pay up, or be left stranded in the middle of nowhere. It was a moment where the wrong answer could've ended badly—and somehow— I navigated my way out.

I've been in situations where I had to physically fight off a man who followed me back to my hotel room—someone who stalked me with the intent to do harm. He tried to strangle me, to overpower me, and assault me. It brought back memories of what happened to me when I was five years old in Vietnam. From that moment on, I promised myself I would never let anything like that happen again. So, I fought—fully aware that it could cost me my life—but I fought anyway. It was a moment that burned itself into my memory, not just for the fear, but for the realization of how vulnerable I truly was, traveling alone in a place where no one would hear me scream.

It wasn't just a close call. It was a fight for my life. And the fact that I'm still here to talk about it is something I'll never take for granted.

**

But danger isn't always overseas. Back in high school, I found myself caught up in the wrong crowds, drawn to the thrill of rebellion, tagging along with the so-called "cool" kids. That pursuit of excitement landed me in not one, but *two* separate shootouts. I wasn't a gangster—I was far from one. I wasn't looking for trouble. I was just a teenage girl chasing a sense of belonging, following boys into places I had no business being in.

It started with a friend inviting me to a party in a part of the city I had no business being in; a neighborhood with a reputation for trouble. I didn't think much of it at the time. I was young, curious, and honestly just wanted to hang out. That night ended in chaos. What began as a party turned into panic when gunshots rang out. I found myself caught in the middle of my first shootout; terrified, confused, and completely unprepared for what was happening around me.

The second time wasn't much different in terms of how it unfolded—except— it was even more surreal. I was tagging along with another friend who used a fake ID to buy liquor. She pulled into a gas station located in an area known for drug activity and gang violence. Because we thought that stores like this would be more lenient with identifying whether her fake id was real or not. I waited in the passenger seat, bored and unaware. As she walked inside, I noticed a commotion gathering nearby—yelling, a crowd forming. Suddenly, a fight broke out on the street beside the gas station we were at, and within seconds, guns were drawn. I heard gunshots…more than one, from more than one person. The crowd scattered like a wave crashing against pavement. My friend bolted from the store, jumped into the car, and we peeled off as fast as we could.

I'm not proud of those moments. I didn't grow up seeking out danger, but somehow it found me anyway. Partly because I followed others blindly, partly because I didn't yet understand the value of self-preservation. Those experiences shook me, left imprints that took years to process. But they also became turning points. They reminded me how quickly things can change; how thin the line is between a typical night out and tragedy.

**

It's easy to look back and shake my head, to ask myself why I didn't walk away. But when you're young and already feel abandoned by the world, danger doesn't always register as danger. Sometimes, it feels like a way to feel alive.

And that's the tragedy of it. I was a kid, starving for love, belonging, and identity. And instead of finding safety, I kept bumping up against the edge of death.

I've danced on the edge more times than I can count. Not because I wanted danger, but because I was chasing connection, escape, experience, or maybe something I couldn't even name. And yet, through every reckless ride and near-miss, something—or someone—always pulled me back from the brink.

**

I say this to myself often— I could fill an entire book with the chaos I've lived through. The mistakes, the dangers I knowingly walked into, and the absolute fuckups I barely crawled out of.

There are chapters of my life I'm not proud of, decisions I made that could've ended everything, times I put myself in harm's way simply because I didn't know better, or maybe didn't care if I made it out. And yet, somehow, I always did.

There's no logical explanation for how many times I've been spared. It's as if something bigger than me, some unseen force or presence, has been keeping watch. I'm not someone who wears religion on their sleeve, but I'd be lying if I said I didn't feel like someone or something out there has had my back all along. There's a certain grace in surviving things you shouldn't have, in still being here to tell the story when every odd was stacked against you.

**

Sometimes I think maybe this is some twisted way for God to make up for the misfortunes and hardships I've faced, offering me protection just to ensure I survive. Or perhaps I have angels watching over me—guiding me through it all. Though I'm not deeply religious, I do find myself wanting to believe in something higher, something that offers guidance during moments of uncertainty. Maybe that's what has carried me through the darkest times…angels, or a higher power, protecting me.

Somehow, maybe even God, saw the confusion and anger in my heart. Because about nine months after the attack in the alleyway in Hanoi, my life took another unexpected turn, one that would change everything forever: I was adopted by two Americans. A couple who chose me not because they had to, but because they wanted to.

It's strange how life works, how it can pull you from despair and place you in the warmth of hope. One moment, I felt as though everything was lost, and the next, I was thrust into an entirely new reality. For the first time, I had a family.

It's hard not to believe that something—or someone—was watching over me during those years. Maybe angels exist, not in the celestial sense, but as the people who step into our lives to guide us when we need it most. My adoptive parents were my angels. They gave me a chance to step into a world I hadn't dared to dream of, one where love, stability, and opportunity were not just distant ideas but tangible realities.

**

I open my laptop. The glow of the screen welcomes me like an old friend. My fingers hover for just a moment before they begin to move. Words flowing more easily this time.

A calmness washes over me as I write, like the storm inside has briefly passed. I no longer feel the need to force clarity or chase meaning. Instead, I just let the story continue, one word at a time. For the first time today, I feel at ease...anchored not by answers, but by the act of sharing a loaf of bread with a street dog.

I take a deep breath, feeling the familiar buzz of caffeine working its way through me. My laptop screen filled with the words I've written, and I can't help but feel a small sense of pride. It's been a journey getting to this point; writing my story, revisiting memories I once thought I'd buried. I pause for a moment, looking up and letting my eyes wander across the cafe.

The people around me are busy with their own worlds: a couple chatting over their coffees, a student typing away on their laptop, a group of friends laughing. The bustle is comforting in its own way. I realize that I've been writing for hours, yet time seems to have slipped away. My mind, so focused on the next part of the story, is now starting to drift. It's been cathartic, letting the words pour out, but now there's a question on my mind: should I head home or stay a little longer to write?

Home seems like the safe option. It's quieter there, more personal, and I can continue writing without the distraction of the cafe around me. But then, I think about how I've been pushing myself lately—pushing myself to heal, to find strength in these words. There's a certain energy here, in this place, among the people who are oblivious to my internal battle. The clatter of cups, the hum of background conversations, the sound of the barista calling out orders; it all feels like a quiet kind of motivation. Maybe I'll stay. Maybe I'll keep writing just a bit longer.

I look back down at my screen, re-reading the last paragraph I typed. It's raw, vulnerable, but it's mine. And that thought, the realization that I've made it this far, fills me with a quiet confidence. There's more to say, more to write, and I know I can do it. I may not have all the answers yet, but the fact that I'm still here, writing, is a victory in itself. So, I decide to stay a little longer.

There's still a lot left to tell.

PHASE 2: Growth

Identity, conflict, growth, discovery

8: Feral Child

When my parents adopted me, I was in rough shape—both physically and emotionally. In every sense, I was a mess. My new family…sister, dad, and mom flew all the way to Hanoi, Vietnam to meet me. I imagine they anticipated a heartwarming introduction and a child with a clean bill of health. Unfortunately, that couldn't have been further from the truth.

The first night with my new family was nothing short of chaotic. I arrived in a fragile state. My body riddled with illness. I had come down with an aggressive case of chickenpox and the flu simultaneously, a painful combination that left me feverish, weak, and barely able to sleep. On top of that, I was severely malnourished. My belly, though bloated, wasn't from food but from a heavy infestation of intestinal worms. My skin was dull, my limbs fragile, and my immune system practically non-existent. I was a medical mess.

My new life in America wasn't an easy transition. I gave my parents hell. I was unsure of my place in this new world. The language was foreign, the food unfamiliar, and the routines felt like stepping into someone else's life, a life I had never known. I wasn't accustomed to the warmth of family dinners, the sounds of laughter echoing through a home, or the constant presence of love. Everything was new, everything was overwhelming. I could feel the weight of the world pressing down on me, but I didn't know how to express the confusion or excitement swirling inside me.

Mowgli

Not only was my health in shambles, but I was also a wild child—untamed, with no understanding of the norms that others took for granted. The concept of toilet paper and modern bathrooms was completely foreign to me. I had spent my life squatting in fields or over holes in the ground. Toilets were strange contraptions, and I had no clue how, or why I was supposed to use them. Chairs and tables were just as perplexing. Everything I ate before adoption had been consumed sitting on the floor, often from shared bowls or makeshift mats. The idea of sitting on a chair and eating at a table was baffling. The ground had been my only constant, a familiar place for everything: eating, sleeping, and living.

Clothing was another mystery. I couldn't grasp why I needed to wear clothes. To me, layers of fabric seemed pointless and restrictive. I was like Mowgli from *The Jungle Book*—wild, unfiltered, and unaccustomed to structure. In every sense, I was a child of the wild, shaped by survival and instinct, not by rules or expectations.

My parents didn't just adopt a child; they opened their home and heart to a small, feral being who had to learn what it meant to live in a world of walls, chairs, clothes, and routines. The transformation wasn't easy, for me or for them.

But what stood out during that chaotic time was my parents' patience. They didn't rush me into anything or expect me to be perfectly healthy overnight. Instead, they took their time, tending to my ailments and showing me the care I had never known. They would hold me when I was feverish, comfort me through my discomfort, and, most importantly, they never gave up on me.

It wasn't easy for them, I'm sure. To take in a sick child like me, would test anyone's strength. But my parents didn't treat me like a burden. They patiently nursed me back to health, one step at a time. They saw my hesitation, the way I clung to the past like a blanket, unsure of how to let go. They didn't rush me to adjust, didn't push me to become someone I wasn't. Instead, they let me be who I was—a girl still learning how to trust, still figuring out how to receive love without fearing it would disappear.

Their love wasn't just a comforting thought; it was in every action, in every careful decision they made to help me heal. It's easy to say that love heals, but for me, my parents' patience, their unwavering support during the worst of my health, showed me that healing is a process. And they were willing to walk through it with me, no matter how long it took. But despite their gentle approach, I wasn't an easy child.

I misbehaved. I was an angry child. A confused one. I acted out in ways that probably left my adoptive parents bewildered and emotionally exhausted. I tested boundaries, not because I was trying to be difficult, but because I was trying to understand what was safe, what was real. I wasn't used to rules, to structure, to the concept of unconditional love. I had never been taught that someone could stay without eventually leaving.

**

In the orphanage, survival had meant adapting quickly and doing whatever it took to get by. That meant staying guarded, learning to fend for myself, and never getting too close to anyone. Affection wasn't something I trusted. It felt foreign, almost threatening. I had learned that love was often followed by loss—and so I carried that shield with me into this new life, this new family.

So much of the fear, habits, and instincts I developed in Vietnam followed me across the ocean, embedding themselves in the corners of my new life in America. One night, not long after I arrived, I wet the bed. It was a simple childhood accident, something many kids experience, but to me, it felt like a catastrophe. I remember waking up in a panic, my body trembling as I stared at the dark stain on the sheets. My heart pounded with fear. I was convinced I would be punished, maybe even hit.

In the orphanage and even before that, accidents weren't just frowned upon, they were met with shame, anger, sometimes even violence. There was no space for compassion, no comfort afterward. Just consequences. So, I tried to hide it. I flipped the blanket. I wiped at the mattress with my sleeve. I panicked, doing everything I could to erase the evidence.

But I think my adoptive parents knew. They had to. The smell, the sheets—it was impossible to completely cover up. Yet they said nothing. There was no yelling, no punishment.

**

I was so disoriented. It took me a long time to adjust to the idea that I wouldn't be punished. I kept bracing myself, waiting for the backlash, the raised voice, the sharp hand. My body was in a constant state of alert, conditioned by years of fear and discipline that had taught me mistakes came with pain. Even when nothing happened, my mind refused to believe it. It was like I couldn't unlearn the instinct to flinch. The safety I was slowly being introduced to felt so foreign, it almost made me uneasy.

When they showed me love, I flinched. When they offered kindness, I tested it. I would act out, withdraw, or erupt in anger—not because I didn't care, but because I cared too much and didn't know what to do with that vulnerability. I pushed back against their affection, against their attempts to connect, as if bracing myself for the inevitable disappointment. As if I could beat them to the punch; push them away before they could abandon me.

Somewhere deep down, I was waiting for history to repeat itself. Waiting for the day they'd decide I was too broken, too much trouble, and walk away. And that fear shaped so much of how I interacted with the world. It wasn't until much later—years into adulthood—that I began to see that these behaviors were rooted not in defiance, but in trauma.

I would slam doors when I was upset, shout when I didn't know how to express my feelings or withdraw into silence when I didn't understand what was happening. I wanted to be loved, but I was terrified to trust it. Every act of kindness felt like it could be a trick, something that would disappear when I least expected it. So, I fought against it.

But again, my parents didn't give up on me. They didn't see my misbehaving as rebellion; they saw it as a cry for help. They understood that I wasn't fighting them—I was fighting the fear of losing something I had only just found. When I pushed them away, they didn't push back—they waited for me to come around. They didn't expect perfection. They didn't expect me to change overnight.

They gave me the space to grow, to heal, and to learn how to trust again. I was given the support I needed to heal and grow. My parents made sure I had access to resources like seeing a child psychiatrist to address my emotional well-being. They also arranged for me to catch up on my education by working with an ESL teacher and keeping track of my progress through regular reports. Most importantly, they created an environment where I felt comfortable, secure, and loved, showing me that they were committed to helping me grow and thrive.

Slowly, over time, I began to understand that love wasn't conditional. It didn't disappear when things got hard. It was constant, steady, and it was mine to receive.

To look back with more clarity, I realize I wasn't a bad kid. I was a hurting kid. A kid trying to survive in a world that had already failed her in too many ways. And while my adoptive family gave me a home, the healing process was slow, and often messy. Because love doesn't erase pain overnight. It just gives it a safer place to land.

**

Looking back now, I realize how much my parents taught me simply by being there, by being patient. They showed me that it was okay to be broken, to be messy, to not have everything figured out. They didn't want a perfect child; they just wanted me. Still to this day, they accept me for me. In fact, it's a running gag in my family that I hold the championship belt for being the "unstable, disgraceful child"—a title I've embraced like a badge of honor. I've turned it into an art form, really. I frequently send my parents memes about moving back in with them as a woman in her 30s, complete with dramatic captions and crying-laugh emojis. They laugh (nervously), I laugh (not-so-nervously), and deep down… I kind of mean it.

My mom usually rolls her eyes in a way that says, "Not again", while my dad just stares off into the distance like he's buffering. Still, I know—without question—that if I ever did show up at their doorstep, bags in hand, spiraling, and all, they'd let me in. My mom would probably feed me before she even asked what went wrong. That's the kind of unconditional love they've always given me: the kind where I know I'm safe, even when I feel like a complete disaster. And honestly, it's comforting to know that no matter how chaotic life gets, no matter how old I am, there's always a plate of food and a place to land.

9: The Road to Belonging

In America, I began to catch up on the childhood I missed out in Vietnam. My new family gave me life. There were family dinners where laughter echoed off the walls, holidays filled with joy and excitement, and bedtime stories that made me feel safe and seen.

As the years went on, our family of four grew to a family of five when my parents adopted a third child from Russia. My parents made the remarkable decision to adopt three girls from different parts of the world: one from Korea, one from Vietnam (me), and one from Russia. You might wonder what led them down this path of adoption. The answer lies in a tragic turn of events that shaped their journey.

Before adoption was even a consideration, my mother endured years of pain and uncertainty due to complications from endometriosis, a chronic condition that affects the tissue lining the uterus. The severity of her symptoms eventually led to a heartbreaking medical decision: doctors informed her that her uterus needed to be removed. It wasn't just a physical loss; it was the shattering of a dream she had held onto…to carry and give birth to a child. I imagine that kind of news reshapes a woman's entire vision of motherhood.

My parents faced the heartbreaking reality that they wouldn't be able to have biological children. But from this tragedy came a profound and beautiful choice: to build their family through adoption.

Rather than letting loss define them, my parents chose love. They opened their hearts to three children from different backgrounds and cultures, giving us all a chance to belong, to grow, and to thrive. Their decision was a testament to resilience and compassion, showing that sometimes life's most painful events can lead to the most extraordinary new beginnings.

**

When I reflect on my childhood, I realize it was rich in ways that truly mattered. My family wasn't wealthy, but we were comfortably middle class. My parents were hard-working, dedicated people who ensured we had everything we needed and more. My mom was a teacher, and my dad owned his own photography business. Both were hardworking and committed to their professions. We had the freedom to explore, learn, and enjoy life. We took yearly family vacations, adventures that bonded us and exposed us to new experiences. My sisters and I had the chance to participate in any sport or activity we wanted—ice skating, swimming, soccer, dance, field hockey, lacrosse, and gymnastics. There were even private violin lessons for my sister and I, and I spent years playing competitive soccer, a passion that shaped much of my youth.

I always had new clothes, ones that were stylish and well-made. We didn't live extravagantly, but the opportunities my parents provided made me feel wealthy compared to where I had come from. In comparison to the scarcity and struggle of my past, my childhood felt abundant. It wasn't just about material things; it was the love, stability, and freedom to grow that made it extraordinary.

Looking back, I see that my childhood was a gift; a beautiful, secure chapter of my life where I could be a kid, dream big, and explore endless possibilities.

I learned to ride a bike in the driveway of my childhood home, my dad's encouraging cheers ringing in my ears as I wobbled and fell, each time gaining more confidence. My mom—one of the best cooks I know, taught my sisters and I how to bake cookies during our Christmas holidays as I snuck spoonful of dough when I thought she wasn't looking, delighting in the small rebellious pleasure of tasting the sweetness before it was baked into something even better. For the first time, I played dolls and dress-up with my sisters, laughing at how silly we looked in mismatched outfits and pretending to be princesses, superheroes, and adventurers.

I learned to laugh openly, without fear of what might happen next, embracing the joy in life that I had never known. My parents didn't just take me in; they allowed me to live. To live in the fullest sense of the word—to play, to laugh, to stumble and get back up. They didn't just raise me—they gave me the childhood I'd been denied, and with it, a sense of belonging and love that I hadn't even known was possible.

These weren't grand gestures, but they were everything to me. They were proof that I belonged, that I was no longer the girl who had been left behind.

**

Even though I wasn't connected to my adopted parents by blood, I felt as if we shared the same DNA. Our bond went beyond genetics, shaping who I was in ways that felt natural and deeply ingrained. I inherited my dad's sense of humor and his love for art; we could laugh about the same things and appreciate creativity together. From my mom, I absorbed a love for reading and a passion for gardening. We even joked that I "borrowed" her big brown eyes and nose, as if biology had nothing on the strength of nurture and love.

Those little shared quirks and inside jokes made me feel undeniably connected to them. It was proof that family is built on more than just biology. It's built on love, shared experiences, and the way we reflect each other in the smallest, most meaningful ways. My childhood was a beautiful tapestry woven from these connections. It was a time of feeling truly seen, understood, and accepted, a reminder that being chosen was just as powerful as being born into a family.

Through my parents, I discovered what it meant to be part of a family, a real family. Not one bound by blood, but by choice and commitment. They taught me that love isn't about perfection or never making mistakes. It's about showing up, day after day, and choosing each other even when things aren't easy. I didn't just catch up on my childhood, I reclaimed it. I found pieces of myself I didn't know were missing, and for the first time, I felt like I wasn't defined by *almost.* I wasn't almost loved or almost wanted. I was fully, wholly embraced.

**

I truly believe that the only reason I've managed to maintain any semblance of sanity in the midst of all my chaotic, trauma-wired thoughts is because of the love, structure, and stability I experienced after being adopted in America. It's undeniable that early experiences shape us, but it's also true that healing environments can redirect the trajectory of a life once destined for darkness.

You can be born into the worst conditions imaginable, endure unspeakable abuse, and still, with enough support, consistency, and care, rise above it. I'm living proof of that. The guidance I received—the kind that says, *"You matter, your voice matters, your pain matters"*—planted the seeds of healing I didn't even know I needed. Without that, I'm not sure where I'd be today. Probably not here, trying to make sense of it all and turn pain into purpose.

So, while I may not have turned out "perfect," I know with every fiber of my being that the nurturing I received is why I turned out functional... and maybe even a little exceptional. Despite everything, I'm not broken beyond repair. I'm complex, layered, maybe a little damaged—but still someone who follows the law, contributes to the world, and is trying, in my own messy way, to make it a better place.

**

If you ask me whether being adopted magically fixed everything, or if my mind suddenly became stable, or if all the anger, confusion, and chaos in my mind disappeared, the simple answer is no.

Adoption didn't erase the scars or smooth over the years of pain I carried with me. While it brought me love and stability, it also brought with it its own set of challenges—new fears, questions, and emotions that I hadn't learned how to process. The anger didn't vanish, and the confusion didn't just fade away. Becoming part of a family didn't erase the scars—both seen and unseen. The physical marks faded with time, but the emotional ones dug in deeper, always lurking in the back of my mind. The confusion, anger, and hurt that had shaped so much of who I was still lingered, as if embedded into the very fabric of my being.

Adoption, as much as it gave me a second chance at life, brought its own set of challenges. It wasn't the fairytale ending that many expect. It was an intricate process of trying to rebuild trust, learn what it meant to truly belong, and to wrestle with my identity. Questions about my past, my roots, and my worth would follow me for years. How do you truly find your place in the world when your history is a patchwork of trauma, survival, and abandonment?

**

As I've gotten older, I've come to realize that healing isn't a straight line. Some days, it feels like a never-ending struggle, as though I'm trapped in the past, unable to move forward. The weight of it all presses down, and it's hard to imagine a day when the memories won't haunt me. But on other days, there's a flicker of light; a moment where peace seems within reach, and I remember that this journey, though painful, is mine. It's a process, a slow unfolding of who I am, as I come to terms with the pain that once felt unbearable. And in that acceptance, there's strength— strength in embracing the parts of me that I used to hide away, in finding healing within the very things I thought would break me.

This is why I find myself here in Vietnam, seated in a café in Ho Chi Minh, fingers poised over my laptop as I try to put my story into words. The strange thing is, I'm still not entirely sure where it's going or if it even has an ending. I don't know if it will ever come together in a way that makes sense. I don't know if it ever needs to.

There's something both freeing and frustrating about writing like this, about pouring my thoughts into a document with no real destination in mind. Maybe that's how life feels sometimes…a constant process of figuring out where to go, trying to make sense of the journey when the path is far from clear. As I sit here, I wonder if I'm ever truly going to finish this chapter, or if I'll just keep writing, letting it evolve with me. But for now, I'm here, writing— because even if I don't know the ending yet, this is the story I need to tell.

**

"Miss, do you need anything else?"

The words cut through the fog of my thoughts, snapping me back to the present. I blink, trying to reorient myself, and meet the eyes of a new waitress standing by my table. Her polite smile and expectant gaze are a stark contrast to the haze of indecision swirling in my mind. It's late in the afternoon now—the morning hours slipped away unnoticed. The first waitress must have finished her shift or gone on break, and the atmosphere of the café has shifted with the arrival of a new crowd.

I glance around. The quiet hum of earlier has given way to the clinking of silverware, the shuffle of chairs, and low conversations between coworkers and friends. The world outside my head is alive and moving. Rationally, I know I should be moving too. Packing up my laptop, closing this chapter of stillness, and head back to the apartment I've temporarily rented as I navigate through the uncertainties of figuring out my next steps in life. But instead, I remain anchored to my seat, my hands resting idly on the keyboard.

I know what I should be doing…focusing on the business I started last year, figuring out how to turn it into something sustainable, something that makes money. Instead, here I am, sitting in a cafe, tapping away on my laptop, pouring my thoughts into a book that isn't making me a dime. I'm spending money I don't have, trying to create something that might one day heal me, but right now, it's just words.

The irony isn't lost on me—chasing self-healing while ignoring the reality of what I really need to focus on. But sometimes, writing feels like the only way to get out of my own head, even if it costs me. I tell myself this writing is important, soul work, deeply healing… which is true. But also, it's kind of my favorite form of productive procrastination… writing life epiphanies while slowly going broke on iced coffee.

My mind is telling me to leave, to be practical, to take a break from the emptiness of creative stagnation. But my body doesn't listen. I stay put, weighed down by an invisible force I can't fully understand. Maybe it's stubbornness, maybe it's hope that inspiration will return if I just wait a little longer. Or maybe it's the simple need to *not* move, to let this moment stretch on until it reveals something—anything—that I've missed.

**

I nod politely to the waitress and ask for another iced coffee. As she walks away, I find myself staring out the window again, watching people go about their lives, wondering why I feel so unable to go about mine.

The cold coffee arrives, condensation already forming on the cup. I sip it slowly, as if the chill might jolt my mind awake. I close my eyes, inhaling the aroma of coffee and the low hum of chatter around me. With my mind drawing blanks, I find myself drifting back to the movie Apocalypto. I remind myself, don't let this story remain an unfinished project. Don't let it become another "almost." This is the moment to push through, to finish what I've started, to not leave my life's narrative hanging in uncertainty. The sense of urgency stirs inside me, pushing me to act, to make sure this book—my story—doesn't end without closure.

So, I press on and keep writing.

PHASE 3: Search
Confrontation, reconnection, love, truth

10: The Choreography of Hiding

When I was in high school, I came across a quote by Henry Wadsworth Longfellow: *"Every man has his secret sorrows which the world knows not; and often times we call a man cold when he is only sad."* Like the name *Almost,* that line lodged itself deep in my mind and has stayed with me ever since. It perfectly captures the mask I often wear, the quiet walls I've built. People may see me as distant, closed off, or even indifferent. But beneath that exterior lies a sea of emotions—sadness, confusion, memories that I can't always articulate. All my life, I've carried my *almosts* and hidden griefs beneath a composed façade well.

The early years of my life forced me to learn how to hide my emotions. It was a matter of survival, a skill I mastered well—concealing the raw, unprocessed pain, pretending that everything was okay when, deep down, it wasn't. But as time passed, I grew tired of this constant act. I craved an outlet to express the whirlwind of emotions I had kept locked away, but I didn't know how to start.

As a child, my emotions often spoke louder than my words. When I was angry, I'd slam doors or scream, unable to contain the storm within me. Happiness made me overly excitable and impulsive, reacting without restraint. Sadness, on the other hand, drove me into isolation; I'd retreat to my room, shutting out the world. Expressing my thoughts clearly was never easy, and I often felt trapped in my inability to communicate what I truly felt.

**

That's when I discovered journaling. It became my sanctuary, a place where I could pour out everything I couldn't say aloud. Writing allowed me to be unfiltered, honest, and vulnerable, unbound by fear or judgment. It wasn't just a hobby; it became a lifeline. Through writing, I found my voice and, more importantly, began to find myself.

You might wonder how someone can sit for an entire day at a café in Ho Chi Minh City, fingers dancing across a keyboard, writing nonstop. For me, it's a continuation of something I've done since childhood—processing my thoughts through writing. The medium has changed; where there was once a journal, there's now a laptop. But the essence remains the same: the act of turning my jumbled thoughts into words.

My first year in America was overwhelming. I didn't know a single word of English, and the world around me suddenly felt even more isolating than the orphanage I had come from. I remember sitting in classrooms, surrounded by sounds I couldn't make sense of, unable to express myself or connect with the people around me. I felt trapped in my own silence.

That frustration built up quickly. I was angry at the language barrier, angry that I couldn't ask for help or even explain who I was. I had so much I wanted to say—thoughts, memories, questions—but no way to say them out loud. So instead, I began writing. Writing became my way of breathing when speaking felt impossible.

**

It was my mother who handed me my very first journal. I'm not sure if she did it intentionally—perhaps she noticed the simmering anger and frustration I couldn't put into words. Or maybe it stemmed from her own love of books and the written word, and she thought journaling might be a small comfort for me too. Whether it was intuition or coincidence, that simple gesture opened up an entire outlet I didn't know I needed. That journal became my refuge—a safe space where I could release what I couldn't say aloud.

I scribbled down anything I could. Thoughts that didn't make sense to anyone else, broken sentences that didn't follow grammar rules, letters I never sent. But it helped. It gave me power in a world where I felt powerless. Writing became the one place where I didn't feel so lost. It was my outlet, my escape, and slowly, my way of reclaiming my voice.

As a child, when emotions overwhelmed me—anger, confusion, or silence—I didn't have the words to explain what I was feeling. I struggled to communicate, often tripping over my thoughts, my words coming out faster than my mind could organize them. I stuttered when flustered, and my emotions felt like a tangled knot I couldn't unravel aloud.

But on paper, I could find clarity.

Writing became my voice when spoken words failed me.

My journal became my safe space, my alternative to running into the rice fields. It was a place to pour out the emotions I couldn't share with anyone else. I started journaling before I even spoke English, during my first year in America. The entries were messy and disjointed, a mix of messy emotions and unpolished ideas. Even now, I imagine anyone who might read those journals would struggle to follow my train of thought.

My mom, ever sentimental, saved all those journals. I often tell myself I'll read through them someday, but I already know what I'll find: fragments of a young mind trying to make sense of the world. Those moments—scribbling words that didn't always make sense—shaped my love for writing. It's why I can sit in this bustling café, completely immersed in my words, shutting out the world around me. Writing is my therapy, my way of finding peace in chaos…I'd like to say that writing has saved my life in more ways than I can truly explain.

**

I've had the gift of growing up in a home where love was patient and nurturing, where kindness was offered freely, and where I was given the space to grow. And yet—there are still days when I feel like I'm drifting. Moments when the shadows of my past sneak in without warning. When the sting of abandonment, the ache of uncertainty, or the deep-rooted fear of never fully belonging wraps itself around me like a heavy blanket I can't shake off—I write.

Even with all the love I've received, there's still a part of me that wrestles with trust. A part that questions if I'm truly enough—if I'll ever be. And that isn't something that a stable home, or even material success, can simply erase. These wounds live deep. They don't always scream, but they whisper at the quietest times—I write.

On days like this, when the fog of confusion clouds my direction, I turn to the only thing that's always made sense: writing. Writing has become my compass. When I feel adrift, I write. When I feel overwhelmed, I write. Maybe that's why I find myself pouring out these thoughts today. Because I'm uncertain. I'm a little lost. I don't know exactly where I'm going, or what's ahead. But in the stillness of the page, I search for pieces of myself... and slowly, I find them.

**

I take a break from my thoughts and walk to the bathroom. The fan hums softly overhead, the light a little too bright against the quiet of my afternoon. I stand at the sink, staring at my own reflection—hair slightly messy, eyes a little tired from thinking too hard. I run the water, warm and steady, and as I wash my hands, I start talking to myself in the mirror, like I've done a hundred times before.

"Okay," I whisper. "This is the part where the book gets a little heavier."

The next chapters aren't just about me. They're about people I love. People I'd protect with everything in me. Even when it's hard. Even when their flaws make it messy to write about. I breathe deep, letting the water run a second longer than needed, trying to figure out how to begin. How do you write honestly about your family without betraying them? How do you hold truth in one hand and love in the other?

I turn off the faucet, pat my hands dry on the towel, and look at myself again. This is the part of the story where the ground gets softer, shakier. But I know I have to walk it anyway. Because real stories don't skip the hard parts. And love—real love—makes space for the truth.

I leave the bathroom quietly, heart a little heavier but more certain of where the words need to go next.

**

My childhood in America was beautiful. It was filled with love, laughter, and opportunities beyond what I could have ever dreamed of during my early years in Vietnam. But the truth is, childhood doesn't last forever. Children grow up. We become teenagers, and teenagers are often rebellious, defiant, and searching for identity. Those formative years can bring out wounds we didn't know were festering. And the reality is, no family is perfect. Even in the most loving homes, misunderstandings happen, expectations clash, and emotions spiral.

My parents adopted three girls from three different countries, each with our own stories of hardship and trauma. Though we came from different parts of the world, we shared one thing in common: we were abandoned. That abandonment left marks on each of us, scars that often-triggered emotions and behaviors we weren't prepared to face. We were each given a second chance at life, but that didn't erase the pain of the past. The scars we carry don't just vanish because we're in a better place. The past doesn't simply let go of us because life has gotten better. Our traumas have a way of clinging to us, whispering doubt and insecurity when everything seems fine on the surface.

At least this is the case with me.

**

My sisters and I—we came from different corners of the world, each carrying our own scars, our own baggage, but somehow bound together by the invisible threads of fate. My sister Julia's journey is one that sticks with me. She was diagnosed with PTSD and a learning disability, conditions that were born from the chaos of her childhood. She came from alcoholic parents who died from the disease that had defined their lives. When she was adopted, the orphanage lied about her age—saying she was around the same age as me, just six months younger. But the truth was darker. A bone scan showed that she was 2-3 years older than what they'd claimed. This kind of deceit is common in orphanages to make children seem more adoptable. On paper, Julia was just a few months younger, and that meant we were in the same grade, same school, even though we weren't truly the same age.

You'd think that being the same age would draw us closer, but instead, it pushed us apart. Julia and I collided in almost everything. We fought constantly. Her learning disabilities made it difficult for her to navigate social situations. and because of that, it was hard for me to deal with her antics.

My anger and inability to communicate effectively when I needed to, were challenges that clashed deeply with my sister's behavior. Instead of understanding her actions, I would often lash out in frustration, unable to express the tangled mess of emotions I was feeling. This, in turn, made things harder for my parents. They were stuck in the middle of two children with histories of trauma, each struggling to navigate their own pain. We were often at odds; our wounds clashing in ways that neither of us knew how to heal. It wasn't easy for anyone, and the tension in our home reflected the complexity of our lives.

**

But if there's one truth I hold onto… it's my unwavering loyalty and fierce love for my sisters. Maybe that's why everything always felt so intense. Why every argument, every misunderstanding, every moment of distance hit me twice as hard. I didn't just feel the pain—I absorbed it.

I've always been the sister who would do anything crazy for them. The kind who would walk through fire, take the fall, even go to jail if it meant keeping them safe. It might sound dramatic, but it's how I love…with everything I have.

And that's what made things so complicated, especially with Julia. My loyalty to her never wavered, but I didn't know how to balance that devotion with the frustration, confusion, and pain that came up during our teenage years. I didn't know how to fight with her and still feel safe. I didn't know how to hold space for both the love and the anger.

So instead, I held it all in until it boiled over, and by then the damage had already been done. Loving her so deeply without knowing how to navigate the hard parts came at a steep cost—a cost I didn't fully understand until much later.

The Image and the Storm

In middle school, Julia and I gravitated toward completely different worlds. I played soccer, which, at our school, placed me squarely in the so-called "inner circle"—the popular crowd made up of athletes, cheerleaders, and the girls everyone seemed to admire. Julia, meanwhile, was drawn to those on the margins—the kids who challenged authority…who didn't quite fit in, who carried a kind of pain the rest of us didn't understand.

By eighth grade, the distance between us had grown more noticeable. Things began to unravel. Julia was caught stealing from a store, and not long after, she started drinking and experimenting with drugs. It was like watching someone you love drift into a storm you couldn't pull them out of.

At that time, I couldn't understand why my sister chose to surround herself with a crowd of outcasts. My thoughts were narrow and childish because I was caught up in the world of popularity. Being popular was almost like a job to me…something I had to maintain at all costs. It meant adhering to certain standards and expectations, which I felt applied not just to me, but to my sister and even my whole family. I had to make sure we lived up to these ideals. Makeup, fashion, boys, and constantly seeking validation from others were all part of the job description.

My focus was on pleasing everyone else, fitting in, and maintaining an image, even though I felt conflicted inside. I thought that being popular was the key to feeling validated and loved, so I held myself and everyone around me to that unrealistic standard. It wasn't just about friendships—it was about a role I had to play to feel like I mattered.

Back then, I chased clarity in all the wrong ways. I thought if I could just be perfect—always smiling, always agreeable, always polished—then I would be loved. I put so much effort into being the version of myself that I believed others would accept. I saw popularity as a kind of trophy, a validation that I mattered. Silly me…how misguided that thinking was.

Looking back, I realize how shallow and fragile that mindset truly was. I was blinded by appearances, caught up in how things looked rather than how they truly were. With my sister especially, I couldn't see past the surface. I judged too quickly, too harshly. I thought I knew better. I mistook confidence for arrogance, humility for weakness, and I let my insecurities dictate how I saw others.

The truth is, I was still a child in so many ways—immature, unaware, desperate for approval. I wasn't ready to see people for who they really were because I hadn't yet figured out who I was.

That season of my life was filled with false clarity. An illusion of control that only left me feeling emptier. But I can look back on that now with humility, because it taught me something real: that perfection is not the path to connection, and appearances are rarely the full story.

11: When Loyalty Hurts

At school, I strived to be exceptional at everything. I was determined to maintain the image of the popular girl, constantly working to uphold that persona. While I was at my peak—excelling in grades, sports, and even the violin—rumors about my family started to circulate. The whispers about my "crazy" sister followed me everywhere.

They'd ask me questions, almost as if they expected me to explain why she was acting out, as if it was somehow my responsibility to fix her. It made my blood boil. As much as I hated what Julia was doing, hearing people call her crazy made me want to scream. Loyalty was everything to me, especially to my sisters, my parents, and the people I loved. But that loyalty was a double-edged sword. At an age where I was just trying to navigate my way through adolescence, the pressure of defending her to people who didn't understand weighed heavily on me.

It was easier to stay silent, to keep my thoughts hidden, but silence only made the bitterness grow.

**

And then, there was the self-harm. An unspoken scream in the form of scars no one wanted to talk about. Julia wasn't just numbing herself with drugs and alcohol. She was carving pain into her skin, using a razor as both a cry for help and a way to feel something—anything—in the numbness that consumed her. Her self-destruction wasn't random; it was deliberate. It was her way of regaining a sliver of control in a world that had made her feel invisible and voiceless.

Her eating disorders were another manifestation of that same inner torment. Food became the enemy and the comfort, a cycle of bingeing and starving that reflected how out of sync she felt with herself. She obsessed over control, punishing her body for emotions she couldn't verbalize. There were days she wouldn't eat at all. These weren't phases—they were symptoms of something deeper, older, and unresolved.

Watching her struggle felt like witnessing someone drown in slow motion. The cuts on her arms, the hollow way she stared past you, the way her clothes hung off her shrinking frame. I don't think any of it was for attention. It was grief turned inward. Rage without direction. And the scariest part? Most people didn't notice. She wore her pain like armor, covered it with sarcasm and a smile that fooled nearly everyone. But those of us close to her—if we were honest—we saw it.

Pain, when ignored, finds a way to be seen. Julia's body became the canvas for everything she couldn't say out loud.

**

My sister Julia has never been the type to express her emotions openly. Not in the way I try to through writing. I may not always speak my feelings aloud, but I've found a release through words on paper, a kind of emotional reckoning that helps me understand myself. Julia, on the other hand, keeps everything tucked away. She doesn't write, she doesn't talk much about what she's going through, and because of that, I often find myself wondering about the landscape of her inner world.

What did she feel during those formative adolescent years? How did she make sense of the chaos we both lived through? We didn't always see eye to eye growing up, and I know I often misunderstood her. But now, as adults, I look at her with more empathy than judgment. Her past was heavy too—marked by trauma, loss, and confusion—but she handled it differently than I did.

Sometimes I catch myself thinking about what coping strategies she might have developed just to survive. I know my own methods—writing, isolation, overachieving—but Julia's were quieter, more internalized. It makes me realize how grief and pain manifest uniquely in each of us. She may not share her story in the same way, but it doesn't mean she hasn't carried the weight of it all.

**

And then I think about my parents during that time. Two people navigating the unfamiliar terrain of raising adopted children with deep emotional scars, all while trying to build a stable family. They weren't perfect, but they were trying. They were juggling their own responsibilities, their own learning curves, and trying to do right by three daughters who had come from vastly different worlds, carrying pain they couldn't always understand or fix.

It couldn't have been easy—trying to connect with children who didn't yet know how to express what they were feeling, who often acted out or shut down because it was safer than letting someone in. I used to see their efforts as shortcomings, but now I realize they were just doing the best they could with what they had. They provided shelter, opportunity, structure, and love, in their own way, even if it wasn't always spoken in the language I wanted at the time.

Looking back, I understand now that healing doesn't just happen for the adopted child, it's a process for the entire family. My parents weren't just raising kids; they were learning how to parent children who'd already seen the world through broken lenses. And for that, I have a quiet gratitude.

Because I could see how much it was taking out of them. My mom, already thin, lost weight rapidly, and her stress was palpable. She barely slept, constantly worried about Julia. My dad worked more hours, but the toll it was taking on him was obvious. There were talks of sending Julia to a group home, but my parents never pulled the trigger.

**

During this time, Brandi— my older sister by just six months and I grew closer. She was only six months older but due to when our birthdays fell, we were in different grades. We were bonded by shared routines and silent understandings. Both of us were athletes, and our sports gave us a kind of escape; a structured world with clear rules, unlike the unpredictable chaos that sometimes stirred at home. Being part of a team gave us purpose, and the friendships we formed there offered a kind of stability we didn't always feel elsewhere.

Brandi, like me, was part of the popular crowd at school. She had a natural confidence that drew people in, and I often found myself tagging along with her and her friends, pulled in by their energy, their confidence, and the way they seemed to move through the world so effortlessly. That was when I started meeting older boys. Boys who were charming and bold, who knew how to say all the right things. It was thrilling at first, like I was stepping into a new version of myself—someone braver, more desirable, more grown-up.

These older boys who noticed me, who gave me attention, who made me feel like I mattered in ways I hadn't experienced before. Their compliments lit something up inside me—how pretty I was, how graceful I looked playing the violin, how fast I was on the field. These words, though shallow on the surface, reached places in me that had long ached for affirmation. They gave me something I didn't know I was starving for: pride. A sense of worth. A fleeting glimpse of self-esteem I hadn't been able to build on my own.

The attention from these boys made me feel like I mattered, even if only for a moment. It gave me a false sense of control, a temporary high that faded as quickly as it came. Deep down, I knew it wasn't real, not the love, not the acceptance, not the safety I was truly craving. But when you don't know how to express your pain, you reach for whatever might make it stop. I was trying to patch a wound with things that couldn't heal, hoping comfort might come from places that only deepened my confusion.

**

Every day, the world around me felt like it was growing more tangled. Layers of confusion, emotion, and pressure that I was too young to untangle, let alone name. I didn't know how to make sense of what I was feeling, so I chased meaning in the wrong places. I mistook attention for love, and silence for strength. I hid my pain behind laughter, behind late nights, behind stories I made up to cover the truth.

At home, things felt heavy. So, I ran. Not physically, but emotionally. Like the rice fields I once escaped to as a child, I disappeared into the safety of my friends, of being out and gone. I told my parents I was sleeping at someone's house, when in reality I was meeting boys, looking for a kind of connection I didn't yet understand. A kind of validation I couldn't find at home.

And what's strange—what stings a little now—is that I used to judge my sister Julia for the way she acted. For how she rebelled, how she sought out her own version of love and attention. But looking back, I see it clearly: I was casting judgment from inside my own messy glass house. I was so quick to throw stones, never realizing the cracks forming in my own walls.

The Night that Broke me

One evening in middle school, I came home from a soccer game to flashing red and blue lights in front of our house. Cop cars lined the driveway. Police officers moved in and out of the front door with leashed K9s, speaking into radios, their boots heavy on the hardwood floors. I stood frozen on the front lawn, my cleats still caked in mud, as neighbors peeked through their windows, whispering behind curtains.

Inside, it felt like time had cracked open. I remember my stomach sinking when I heard why they were there: Julia had told someone at our school that she had a gun in the basement and was going to kill our entire family. She specifically said she was targeting me. My name, spoken in that context, stung like ice. I couldn't understand it. I was thirteen. I was just a kid trying to make the JV soccer team, trying to pass math, trying to be enough.

They showed us drawings she had made…sketches in her journal of me being decapitated. I stared at them blankly. I didn't cry. I didn't scream. I didn't say a word. The hatred she felt toward me was so sharp, so personal, I didn't know where to place it. I didn't even have the language to process it.

**

Something changed in me that night. Something inside me snapped. Not in a loud or visible way, but in that quiet, terrifying way where the body remembers what the mind tries to forget. I reverted back to the five-year-old girl in the orphanage—the one who would lay still at night, refusing to cry, refusing to speak, holding in every scream. But this time, the dissociation came with something different: rage.

It wasn't just numbness. It was fire locked behind my ribs. I floated above my body, going through motions while this weight, this fury, simmered beneath the surface. I became detached from the world around me, but hyper-aware of every threat. I couldn't always explain what I was feeling—I just knew I was on edge, waiting for the next betrayal, the next moment I'd have to survive.

People saw me functioning and thought I was fine. But they couldn't see the version of me curled up on the inside, fists clenched, eyes wide open. The little girl who used to lay in silence was back—but this time, she wasn't scared. She was furious.

**

I had always felt like I was chosen for bad things—chosen to be the one beaten by my aunt in Vietnam, chosen to be abandoned and sent to an orphanage, chosen to be attacked on the streets of Hanoi. And now, once again, I was the "chosen one" to be targeted by my own sister. The psychological damage of that night only deepened my already fragile sense of self. My mind, which had already been fractured by years of trauma, was now pushed further to the brink.

I stopped caring about a lot of things. School didn't feel important. Friends felt distant. Even soccer, and the violin, which had once been my escape, started to feel pointless. I went through the motions, but I wasn't really there. I stopped trying to explain myself to the world. I stopped expecting people to understand or protect me.

It was the moment I started building walls without realizing it. Emotional ones. Ones that said, "Don't get too close," even when all I wanted was to be held. To be safe.

But even in the midst of all the confusion and anger, one thing became clear to me—the silence I had once learned to endure was no longer enough. My anger had finally found its voice. And in that voice, I started to question everything—my past, my family, my role in all of it. The anger I had been holding in for so long started to come out at home.

I screamed at my parents, talked back to them, and lost interest in things I used to love. Life at home felt suffocating, and I began to resent the very people I had once been so loyal to.

What hurt more than the drawings or the police notifying my family Julia's plan, was the silence that followed. No one wanted to talk about it. It became the elephant in the room. My parents did what they thought was right—they found a counselor, set up therapy sessions, tried to help me process everything. We bounced around from therapist to therapist, but I couldn't connect with any of them. I was angry—raw, volatile, inconsolable. I spent most sessions either silent or screaming. And the ones where my mom sat in with me? They turned into battlegrounds. Not quite conversations. Not healing moments. Just shouting—mostly from me.

**

After the gun incident, I found myself in yet another situation that reflected just how lost I was at the time. I started dating a guy who, in hindsight, was completely wrong for me. But in my rebellious state, I saw him as exciting; someone who understood the chaos in me. One afternoon, he came over and sat with me in the backyard. My sister Julia was there too. He knew about the recent trauma—the gun incident—and instead of being respectful, he taunted her, pushing every emotional button he could.

Julia, who had been holding in so much pain and rage, finally snapped. She stormed into the kitchen, grabbed a knife, and chased him down the street. It was a terrifying scene. I called the police, and once again, a swarm of officers showed up to deescalate the situation—just like they had before.

That evening turned into a battleground inside our home. I lashed out at my parents, screaming, blaming them, defending the boyfriend who had no business provoking my sister. I was blinded by what I thought was love. I couldn't see at the time that he had crossed a line. Instead, I saw only my sister's outburst and my parents' disapproval, and I turned my anger on them.

**

I was furious. Not just about what happened with Julia, but about everything. The chaos, the pain, the injustice of it all. I felt betrayed—by my family, by the silence, by how quickly everything had spun out of control. In my mind, I was the one who got hurt. I was the victim. And yet, it felt like my pain was being handled with soft gloves, like it was too inconvenient to deal with head-on.

What burned most was the feeling that Julia wasn't being punished enough; that no one was taking my fear seriously. I wanted someone to be held accountable. I wanted justice. And when I didn't get it, I turned my rage inward and outward. I blamed everyone around me, especially the people closest to me. I couldn't see their hurt because mine felt louder. I was so lost in my own grief that I couldn't make room for theirs.

I was so consumed by my own anger that I couldn't see the pain my parents were carrying. At the time, I didn't have the capacity—or maybe the willingness—to look beyond my own grief. But now, with maturity and time, I can begin to imagine it: two kind, loving souls trying their best to hold together a house with three daughters, each one hurting in her own way, each one expressing it differently. It must have felt impossible.

I think about them now and wonder how they managed to get up every day, to go to work, to cook dinner, to smile through the tears, to juggle the weight of everything crumbling behind closed doors. They were doing the best they could in the middle of a storm no one saw coming. But back then, I couldn't see any of it. I couldn't see past my own rage. I was too hurt to see theirs.

**

I wish I had known how to extend grace to my parents in those moments. I wish I had known that they were hurting too; confused, scared, probably just as lost as I was. But in my young mind, I was the one wronged. I couldn't understand the complexity of it all. I just wanted someone to blame, and my anger needed a place to land.

Looking back, I know now that pain doesn't exist in isolation. Everyone was hurting. Everyone was surviving the only way they knew how. I just wish I could have understood that sooner. I now know that therapy wasn't failing me—I was just too deep in my anger to let it help. I didn't want to be helped. I wanted to be seen. I wanted someone to stand up and say, "You didn't deserve this." But when no one did, I screamed it myself. Over and over again. Until I didn't have the energy anymore.

**

As much as I hated everything about Julia during that time—her actions, her words, the chaos she brought into our lives—there was still something buried deep within me that pulled at the threads of loyalty. That unspoken bond of shared sisterhood. That invisible string that refused to fully break, no matter how hard I tried to sever it.

It was confusing, even painful. But that pull is what made me pause. It's what made me try, however reluctantly, to understand her. To see her side. I didn't want to. I didn't want to give her the grace I felt she hadn't earned. But part of me couldn't help but wonder why. Why she was the way she was. Why she hated me. Why she did the things she did. I didn't get many answers, but I needed to ask the questions anyway.

So, I wrote. A lot.

There are pages and pages of journal entries during that time—raw, desperate scribbles of a sister trying to make sense of the unexplainable. I asked the same questions over and over, not because I expected my journal to respond, but because writing felt like the only safe place I could have the conversation. I poured out anger, confusion, guilt, and—though I didn't want to admit it—longing. Longing for something better between us. For clarity. For closure. Maybe even for connection.

But the truth is, I didn't find an answer. Not then. Maybe not even now. Still, I kept writing. Because somehow, even in the absence of answers, writing helped me survive the not knowing.

**

As my spiral into isolation deepened, I couldn't help but blame Julia for all of it. It was easier that way—easier to point my finger at the one who'd hurt me most, the one whose actions cracked something in me that I didn't know how to repair. I began shutting people out, retreating further and further into my own head. I avoided friends, skipped family dinners, and spent hours alone in my room just to feel a sliver of control.

In my eyes, Julia had set everything on fire and left me to sit in the ashes. The loneliness, the fear, the constant ache in my chest. I tied it all back to her. I carried that resentment like armor, believing it protected me. But really, it only pushed me further away from everyone else. I was angry, yes—but beneath that anger was grief. A quiet, raw grief for the sister I never really got to have, and the version of myself that I lost in the chaos.

Blaming her gave me a focus, something to direct all the hurt toward. But the more I held onto that blame, the more I realized, it wasn't healing me. It was just keeping me stuck.

I selfishly wanted to make myself feel better by blaming her for my downward spiral, for my family's reputation, my parents struggle—she had tarnished it all. I had been the popular girl at school, admired by my peers for my grades, my sports achievements, and my friendships. But then, Julia came along with her problems, dragging my family's name through the mud. I felt like she had sabotaged everything I had worked so hard for.

Every day felt like a battle. Going to school became unbearable. The whispers in the hallways, the constant questions about my "crazy sister," they only made my anger burn brighter.

Whenever someone asked, "How's your sister?" or "Is she still crazy?" I would lash out. I couldn't take it anymore. It felt like I was trapped in a nightmare that I couldn't escape. My frustration at home only deepened as the burden of everything became too much to bear.

After Julia's gun incident, my parents decided it was time to send her to a group home for troubled teens. There, she stayed, enduring her ups and downs while I stayed behind, dealing with my own battles.

9th Grade

My freshman year of high school was the beginning of my downward spiral. Things began to unravel for me. I lost friends because I felt people didn't understand me anymore. I blamed everyone but myself. I became more selfish. My room became my sanctuary. I would stay up late, staring at the ceiling, lost in thoughts I couldn't express. I finally found a counselor that understood my feelings, but even those sessions couldn't erase the feeling that my life—my reputation—was ruined.

I blamed Julia for everything. I blamed her for my loss of interest in soccer, for the friends I had lost, for the grades that took a toll on my schoolwork, and for the depression that now consumed me. It wasn't just about her anymore, it was about everything falling apart.

I became increasingly isolated, more withdrawn. I continued to hang out with older guys and people who didn't care about consequences. Ironically, I was doing the same thing that I couldn't understand why Julia was doing. I lied to my parents, sneaking around, pretending I was fine when I wasn't. My anger reached a boiling point, and instead of talking about it, I lashed out at the people who loved me the most: my parents. I wanted them to feel my pain, my frustration, because I couldn't express it in any other way.

10th Grade

Things got worse during my sophomore year when my other sister, Brandi, became pregnant. She had a baby during her junior year of high school, and that put our family under an even harsher spotlight. Once again, our family's problems became the talk of the town. I was targeted. I became the end of cruel taunts and bullying. Racist comments were thrown at me in the hallways, and I was called all sorts of names—because people at my high school couldn't get to my sisters, they picked on me. I took it, like I had taken everything else in my life. It wasn't the first time I had been hurt, and it wouldn't be the last.

I lost more friends, but I didn't care. By that point, I lost interest in almost everything that once brought me joy. My high school years became a haze of depression and unresolved anger—an anger I didn't know how to process or express in any healthy way.

I turned inward. Isolation was my constant companion. I grew more depressed, but I kept it to myself. I didn't want to burden my parents with my pain, so I would often lie about being sick to avoid school. I took the long way home from school, winding through back streets and side paths, just to avoid being seen by other students. It wasn't just about not wanting to talk—it was about hiding. I didn't want the stares, the awkward hellos, the possibility that someone might ask how I was doing when I didn't even know the answer myself.

I've always had a way of finding hidden trails—quiet, tucked-away places where I could retreat into my own world. As a child in Vietnam, it was the rice fields: vast, open stretches where I could disappear into the silence and feel like the world paused just for me. After moving to America, that instinct didn't change. I found a narrow, lesser-known path that cut between buildings and wove through trees on my walk home from school. It wasn't the fastest route, but it became my sanctuary.

That walk became my daily escape route, a quiet ritual of avoidance that, in its own way, brought a small sense of control in a time when everything else felt like it was slipping through my fingers.

But nothing could escape the anger I held inside. It kept building, with no place to go. The frustration, the hurt, the confusion—it all boiled over into an unbearable rage I couldn't shake. And so, I kept it in, hiding behind my silence, my isolation, as the world around me continued to fall apart.

**

The thoughts that filled my journal during these years were clouded by pure hatred and anger. I became consumed with bitterness, constantly blaming everyone around me for my problems, while I remained untouched by any fault. I couldn't see the toll my behavior was taking on my family. My mom, weighed down by the stress of managing three teenage girls, was visibly losing weight, but I couldn't bring myself to care.

My dad, already distant, seemed even more absent as I spiraled deeper into my own world of anger. My dad started staying at work longer and longer hours. At first, I thought it was just a heavy workload or his desire to avoid the chaos at home, but as time went on, I began to realize there was more to it.

One day, my mom told me the truth: he'd been drinking at his office. Not a single beer to wind down, not just a glass of wine to take the edge off—a routine. It became his own silent escape, his own coping mechanism for a world he couldn't control. And honestly, I was shocked. He had always carried himself with such composure, such restraint. But underneath that surface was a man unraveling quietly, privately.

It broke something in me. Not just the image I had of my father, but the realization that everyone in our house was fighting battles no one else could see. I had been so wrapped in my own anger, in my own pain, that I didn't see his. I didn't see how hard it must have been for him to watch his daughters drift away from each other, from him, and from the life he once worked so hard to provide.

Looking back now, I realize that his absence wasn't just physical—it was emotional too. And maybe that was his way of surviving. Maybe we were all just doing whatever we could to make it through each day, even if it meant disconnecting, numbing, or running away.

**

"Miss, can I get you another coffee?"

I look up, startled. Two hours have passed since I last looked up to take a breather. The café, once bustling with the lunch crowd, has grown quiet. It's just me and one other person now, a few tables away, absorbed in their own world. I glance at the waitress, nod, and order another coffee. At this point, I don't even need the caffeine, but the act of sipping something while I write has become part of the routine, the habit I've fallen into.

As the waitress walks away, I feel a flicker of annoyance. I was in the middle of a thought, a place where words flow freely, and now I've been interrupted. But then I pause. Maybe this is a sign to step back, to take a break. There's a small wave of anger that rises in me, as I begin to think about that phase of my life—the one I'd rather leave behind. It's funny how, no matter how much time has passed, past incidents can still stir up emotions. The simplest memory can still make you feel something, even when you've convinced yourself that you've moved on.

I know deep down that this might be the reason I've been stalling on writing this book. I'm scared. Scared of being vulnerable. But vulnerability, I remind myself, can be a good thing. Maybe it's the only way forward.

Writing, after all, is about exposing the parts of yourself you'd rather keep hidden. The things you'd prefer to forget. And yet, it's in these raw moments that I find my truth, the words that give shape to my past. Even though it hurts sometimes, maybe it's the only way to heal.

12: First Love

I sit back in my chair, letting my eyes wander for a moment as I wait for the waitress to bring over my coffee. The clinking of mugs and the low hum of chatter float around me, a kind of white noise that gives my thoughts space to breathe.

High school. It hits me how much of that time I've spent trying to forget. So much anger, so much hatred toward everything—toward myself, toward my family, toward the world. But what I rarely talk about, what even I forget sometimes, is that those years weren't only filled with pain. There was love too. Real, powerful, love.

I met my first love during that time. A kind of gentle refuge from the chaos I was living in at home. He saw something in me, something I didn't even see in myself. And for the first time in a long time, I felt seen. Understood.

That love gave me something to hold onto when everything else felt like it was falling apart. It helped me cope. It helped me heal, even if only in small ways. And maybe that's what love does best—not fix you, but make the pain feel just a little bit more survivable.

The barista sets the coffee down gently in front of me. I nod, mumble a quick thank you, and wrap my hands around the iced coffee that has already melted. I take a sip and smile faintly to myself. Love saved me, once. Maybe it still does.

**

Love. That word alone holds a universe. It's delicate, yet powerful. It's been both the soft place I fall into and the fire that's refined me. Love has been the light that pulled me out of the darkest corners of my life. It's because of love that I flourished in the care of my adoptive parents—the kind of unconditional, intentional love that doesn't ask for anything in return but still gives everything. Their love taught me what safety feels like, what it means to be chosen, to be wanted. It allowed me to start seeing the good in people, even when I had every reason not to.

It's love that gives me the strength to sit in this café right now, reflecting on trauma that once left me feeling broken beyond repair. Even in anger, even in grief, there's a gentleness now that wasn't there before. That gentleness is love. A calmer version of myself is starting to emerge— not because the past has disappeared, but because love has helped me hold it differently. I'm healing, slowly, but with love in my corner.

**

There are two kinds of love that shaped me deeply, and the first one I want to talk about is my first real love—Eric. He came into my life my sophomore year of high school—at a time when I felt like everything around me was falling apart. I was young, wounded, and angry. I didn't understand my place in the world. But Eric, he didn't try to fix me. He simply showed up. Steady. Present. His love wasn't loud or dramatic. It was quiet, like a steady heartbeat. He made me feel seen in a way I hadn't felt in years.

He reminded me that I could be lovable, even when I was angry, closed off, or pushing people away. Even when I built walls so high that most would give up trying to climb them, he stayed. He didn't flinch when I lashed out. He didn't walk away when I grew cold or distant. He stood there, quietly, and patiently, reminding me through the small things—through gentle texts, warm glances, late-night talks—that I wasn't broken beyond repair.

He showed me love in the moments I felt most unworthy of it. When I was drowning in guilt, in self-loathing, in confusion about who I was and where I belonged, he chose to see the parts of me I had buried. The girl who still wanted to be understood. The girl who still believed in connection, even if she was afraid of it. His presence was not loud or demanding; it was consistent. It was kind. And in a time when I didn't even like myself, he helped me believe that I could still be loved—not for who I pretended to be, but for who I really was.

And that changed something in me. It softened the sharp edges, just enough for me to breathe again. Just enough to make space for healing.

Eric was everything I didn't know I needed. He was three years older than me—older, wiser in some ways, and the complete opposite of everything I was used to. Grounded, soft spoken, and easygoing. He came from a warm, structured family. A sharp contrast to my chaotic household. And yet, we clicked. We didn't have the same backgrounds, but we shared something that transcended all that: comfort. I didn't have to perform or pretend. I could just be. He gave me something so rare: a soft, peaceful chapter in the middle of a turbulent story.

**

I had boyfriends before, of course. But Eric? Eric was different. He wasn't just a high school crush. He was my first real love—the kind of love that makes you feel safe enough to exhale for the first time in years. He didn't try to fix me. He just accepted me. And in that quiet, steady way, he gave me what I needed most during that chapter of my life: peace.

Eric entered my life at a time when everything felt fragile—like the world around me could crack at any moment. I didn't realize it then, but love, especially a gentle love, can be a kind of lifeline. He didn't swoop in with grand gestures or try to pull me out of the mess I was navigating; he simply existed beside me. A presence. A comfort. And in the madness of high school hallways, family struggles, and inner battles I couldn't yet name, he gave me a reason to breathe a little easier.

Eric and I had a natural rhythm together. Our personalities just clicked. We shared a deep love for sports; he was athletic, and watching games together became one of our favorite pastimes.

Whether it was basketball, football, or even something new we hadn't seen before, we were always up for the energy of a live event.

Our bond extended beyond the stadium. We had the same taste in food—Chinese, Thai, anything with bold flavors—and we both had adventurous palates, always looking for the next dish to try. Traveling was another shared joy. Exploring new places side by side brought out the best in both of us. We'd dive into the culture, try the local food, and create memories in places we'd never been before.

Even our downtime felt effortless. We liked the same types of movies, from thrillers to comedies, and never struggled to decide what to watch. Being around Eric didn't require effort or performance. It was easy, light, and comfortable. We just fit. Being with him felt like being seen and accepted in the most uncomplicated, genuine way.

Eric and I shared a deep love for music, and that connection ran as strong as all our other shared passions. We had the same taste—90s and early 2000s rap, artists like Nas, Biggie, Jay-Z. 90s alternative rock like the Goo Goo Dolls or Red Hot Chili Peppers. It wasn't just casual listening; we both felt the lyrics, the rhythm, the storytelling. Music wasn't background noise—it was a shared language between us. He had this incredible ear for beats and transitions because one of his hobbies was DJ-ing. I remember how I used to scroll through his playlists and let them shape my own taste. Truthfully, a lot of my current music inspiration comes from him. His playlists were the soundtrack to our road trips, lazy Sundays, and late-night conversations.

**

He had these striking blue eyes that seemed to glow even more against the contrast of his dark brown hair. His eyelashes were long and thick—not in a way that made him look feminine, but rather added a depth to his gaze that was quietly magnetic. There was something about the way he looked at you—intense, thoughtful, a little mysterious. I used to tease him that he should be a model, not just because he was handsome, but because that look—the way his eyes could hold yours—had a presence. It wasn't just physical beauty; it was the quiet confidence and stillness behind his stare that made it unforgettable.

And he wasn't just creative—he was brilliant. Quietly so. He never flaunted it, but he was smarter than most people I'd ever met. He had this calm, thoughtful way of speaking, with a soft-spoken voice that drew people in. There was something so steady about him, a kind of internal peace that made him incredibly grounding to be around.

In the nearly six years we were together; not once did he ever raise his voice at me. That kind of consistency and emotional regulation is rare. His calming nature became a refuge for me. He wasn't just my partner; he was a sense of safety in human form. In a world that often felt chaotic and overwhelming, Eric was the stillness I didn't even know I needed.

**

But our differences were obvious…he was put together and had a certainty in life that I envied. He talked about college, about his parents' love story, about faith and tradition. I was the girl who flinched at the word trust, who couldn't talk about her past, who didn't know what she believed in. But somehow, those differences made the connection stronger. With Eric, I could show up exactly as I was—wounded, guarded, raw—and he never asked me to be anything more or anything less.

He saw past the anger and confusion I sometimes carried like a shield. He saw the girl who wanted to be held and told everything would be okay. He didn't need to fix me. His love wasn't flashy—it was warm, consistent, and patient. Sometimes we'd sit in his car after a sports game, not even saying anything, just holding hands while the music played. And in those quiet moments, I felt more understood than I ever had before.

**

There are certain people who enter our lives and, even if they don't stay, their presence lingers like the warmth of a fire long after it's gone out. Eric was that for me. He was more than a high school and college boyfriend—he was a kind of refuge, a reminder that I was capable of being loved in a healthy, stable way. I didn't have to prove anything to him. I didn't have to pretend. For once, someone wasn't trying to control me, fix me, or dismiss me. He simply saw me.

We had the kind of relationship that felt like a deep breath—steady and necessary. Eric taught me what it meant to be emotionally safe with someone, even when I didn't have the language to explain my trauma. He didn't interrogate my pain, he didn't push for answers, but he offered space. He gave me the gift of quiet mornings, and a kind of unwavering presence that made everything else feel a little less heavy.

There were moments I wanted to run; because that's what I was used to doing when things got too calm or too close. But Eric never chased me. He waited. He waited until I came back, until I was ready to sit beside him again. That kind of patience left a mark on me deeper than any apology I'd ever longed for from my past.

Because of my relationship with Eric, something inside me slowly began to shift. Being around him gave me space to breathe, to be a teenager again—without the constant weight of resentment or the pressure of survival.

**

We ended because we simply outgrew each other. Life moved on. College, distance, time; it all had its way of reshaping us. But even now—years later—I sometimes wonder if he knew just how much he helped save me during those fragile years. I wonder if he knew that in a world where I didn't always trust love, his was the one I believed in. He showed me it didn't have to hurt.

And maybe that's why I still carry a soft spot for him—not out of longing— but out of gratitude. Because in the middle of my story, in a chapter filled with confusion, Eric was the calm. And sometimes, that's all a person needs to make it through.

While we've long since gone our separate ways, there's a corner of my heart where his memory lives gently. He was a calm in the storm, and no matter where life takes me, I'll always be grateful that our paths crossed when they did. Because sometimes, love doesn't need to last forever to leave an everlasting imprint.

13: First Heartbreak

There are some kinds of love that don't fit neatly into the boxes we're taught as children. There's the kind of love that feels safe. The kind that's loud and celebratory. And then there's the quiet kind—the complicated kind—the love that, from the outside, looks like a mistake. But to me, this love was real, deep, and formative. This love was my first and only heartbreak, but it was also one of the most powerful teachers of my life.

I met him while in law school—at a time when my world was crumbling. I was failing in class, doubting my worth, wondering if I had made the biggest mistake trying to chase this impossible dream. I felt like a fraud sitting among my peers, who all seemed to carry the confidence and clarity I lacked. And then, there he was: this man with beautiful blue eyes and a presence so calm, it softened the chaos in my mind.

He wasn't just anyone, he was someone important. Respected. Successful. Older. And yes—married.

**

He was married. And I knew what I was walking into. I won't make excuses; I'm not here to defend my choices. At the end of the day, I knowingly stepped into a relationship with a married man, and that alone carries its own weight of judgment. In truth, this wasn't an ideal situation, and I take full responsibility for my part in it. But relationships aren't always black and white, and not every marriage is what it seems from the outside.

I didn't go into this blindly. I chose to be there, even knowing what he was tied to. And while I understand how complicated and flawed that choice was, it was my reality at the time.

Our connection wasn't something I planned. It wasn't something I had ever dreamed of. It just happened. At first, I resisted. I judged myself harshly for being involved with a married man, something I swore I'd never do. I held tight to the values I was raised with, and family has always meant everything to me. I knew what it felt like to come from brokenness, to long for stability, and I hated the idea that I could be contributing to someone else's pain.

The guilt sat in my chest like a stone, and yet, the connection we had was undeniable. It wasn't rooted in lust or some reckless thrill, it was a bond built over long conversations, emotional vulnerability, and mutual respect. He wasn't just a married man to me. He was someone who truly saw me, who treated me with kindness and humility. He valued my thoughts, my perspective, even when I didn't have everything figured out.

Some might assume he took advantage of my vulnerability, or that a married man had no business stepping outside the boundaries of his marriage. And I understand why people would think that; it's a fair judgment from the outside looking in. But life, especially relationships, is rarely black and white. Marriage, in all its complexity, often holds layers that aren't visible to anyone outside the partnership. It's easy to draw conclusions from a distance, but the truth is, not every situation fits neatly into right or wrong.

I'm not excusing anything. I've wrestled with my own guilt, my own accountability. But I also know that what unfolded between us didn't stem from manipulation or malice. It came from a genuine connection that neither of us expected. And sometimes, life puts people in your path in the most complicated, imperfect ways.

**

We lived in different states. But somehow, that distance didn't feel so wide. Because we talked every single day. Sometimes, it felt like I was right there next to him, like we shared a quiet corner of the same room even if we were hundreds of miles apart.

He shared with me everything—his deepest vulnerabilities, the wounds from his past, the details of his present, and the hopes he held for his future. There was nothing surface-level about our conversations. He wasn't just a romantic partner; he became my best friend. The kind of best friend you don't expect, the kind who somehow makes the world feel less heavy.

He traveled frequently for work, often hopping from one city to another, sometimes even internationally. A few times each month, he'd fly me out to wherever he was, and those trips became our little adventures. We had so much in common, especially when it came to food. Wherever we went, we made it a point to find the best steakhouses in town, turning every dinner into something memorable. We also shared a love for hockey, which gave us something fun and familiar no matter where we were.

He was incredibly easygoing and traveling with him never felt stressful. He had this way of making everything feel seamless and calm. Whether we were flying from one state to another, or boarding a plane overseas, it always felt like an exciting escape—never a chore. Traveling together didn't just reveal new places; it showed me how compatible we were in unfamiliar environments, how naturally we moved through the world as a pair.

**

I was also deeply drawn to the kind of father he was. There was something incredibly attractive about the way he spoke about his children—with warmth, pride, and such attentiveness. In our conversations, he would often speak about his children with a kind of warmth and pride that softened his whole demeanor.

He would tell me stories about his kids. Little details about their personalities, the things they loved, the moments that made him proud. And even though I wasn't physically part of their lives, I found myself growing attached to them through those stories. I cheered them on from afar, quietly hoping for their happiness and success, because family has always meant everything to me.

It gave me insight into his values, his patience, and the kind of man he was at his core. He wasn't just successful or charming, he was nurturing, and that added a depth to him that I hadn't seen in many others. Listening to him talk about his children felt like listening to someone describe their heart walking around outside of their body. I could feel the love that bound them together.

**

He was also brilliant. He was older, but you wouldn't have known it from the way we connected. We shared similar values, a matching sense of humor, and a deep appreciation for the smaller, quieter moments in life. Some of the funniest, most ridiculous memories I carry happened with him—just the two of us laughing until we cried over something totally unimportant.

He let me into spaces most people keep hidden. And because of that, I saw sides of him that maybe no one else did. The way he carried the weight of responsibility, the quiet sadness he tried to mask with humor, the pressure of being everything to everyone. And still, through it all, he gave me parts of himself that made me feel seen, understood, and appreciated.

And despite all of his accomplishments, the money, the experience, the life he'd already lived— he never made me feel less than. In fact, he would turn to me for advice. He sought out my opinion, genuinely listened to my perspective, and treated my thoughts with weight. For someone who was still in school, still figuring out who I was, that meant everything. He saw me not just for what I was in that moment, but for who I could become. And that kind of respect, that kind of belief—it left a permanent mark on me.

It's strange to think about it now…how someone whose life looked so different from mine on the outside, could feel so emotionally aligned with me on the inside.

**

You might look at this and think, *How foolish. You wasted four years of your life on a man who wasn't truly yours.* But if I'm honest, I needed those four years more than I ever thought I would. I was floundering in law school, questioning my every move, doubting if I even had it in me to finish. And then he came into my life—not to save me, but to steady me.

He was a calming presence in the chaos. He allowed me space to cry, to rage, to unravel. I could be myself with him, fully and completely. He never tried to change me—he just listened. He had the kind of listening skills most people only dream of finding in a partner. We would talk for hours, sometimes about nothing, sometimes about everything. His emotional intelligence was off the charts, and when the world felt too heavy, he was the one who helped me carry the weight.

He wasn't just a partner—he became my therapist, my mentor, my sounding board. He supported the same causes I believed in, donated quietly to things that mattered to me, and encouraged me when I didn't have the energy to encourage myself. Despite his success, he was the humblest man I knew. For four years, he was my peace, my comfort, and my clarity. I never went to therapy during that time, not because I didn't need it, but because in him, I found a kind of healing that felt just as powerful.

**

What made this love so complex was that it never claimed to be forever. We both knew this chapter would end. And when it did, it didn't come with bitterness. We parted with grace. We even joked that he would be at my wedding someday—not as my groom, but as someone who had once held my heart with tenderness.

He wasn't the villain in our story—I was the one who broke it off. And it wasn't because I wanted to. I did it because I loved him. Because I respected him. Because I knew what that kind of love required, and I wasn't in a place to give it without destroying everything else. That's what makes it my first real heartbreak. Not the ending, but the quiet, painful truth that I ended something beautiful, not out of hate or betrayal, but out of love.

In the end, it was me who walked away. Yes, we talked about a future together. But it was never really on him to make that choice. I told him not to. We both knew; it was never a question. I value family more than anything. I always have. I spent my early childhood in Vietnam without one, and because of that, I held the concept of family with deep reverence.

I couldn't be the reason someone else's children lost their stability. I couldn't walk into that world and replace what was already complicated. So, I made the decision to let him go.

That's also why I never pushed the topic of divorce. Deep down, I understood it wasn't a real possibility. His life was layered, complex—full of responsibilities and ties I respected, even from the outside. And because I walked into the relationship knowing exactly what it was, the absence of that possibility wasn't a shock to me. It was part of the reality I had already accepted.

**

I kept my first real heartbreak hidden, tucked away like a secret I wasn't ready to explain. To most of my family and friends, I played the role of the carefree, single woman. The one who was always busy, always moving, always laughing. But beneath that mask was a quiet grief I carried alone. I only confided in one sister about him, and even then, I kept things vague. No names. No details. I spoke about him like he was just a passing thought, a guy I once dated, not someone who shook the foundation of how I understood love and permanence.

I never mentioned the word *marriage*. I didn't bring up the fact that he already had children, or that his life was well-established while mine still felt like it was just getting started. Because to use those words would be to invite questions, and judgment, and whispers I wasn't ready to deal with.

Society loves a love story—until it doesn't fit the script. And this love? It didn't fit. It wasn't forever. I knew that even while I was in it. And because of that, I chose to shield it. Not because it wasn't real, but because explaining it would've required more energy than I had. Why open up about something that wasn't built to last? Why expose something tender to people who might only poke at the parts that were already sore?

It was easier, cleaner, to let the world think I was just alone. Not heartbroken. Not mourning something private and powerful. Just alone.

This was my first real heartbreak—not because of the breakup, but because from the very beginning, we both knew we wouldn't last. We were never meant to be a forever. Society wouldn't have allowed it, not with the kind of public reputation he held. He was well known, respected, and carried a name that meant something in certain circles. To walk away from a life he had carefully built for decades—that would've been devastating for him. And I couldn't be the reason he lost all of that.

**

To this day, we still exchange birthday wishes. He still sends advice when I ask. The romantic part may have ended, but the love remains in another form. I owe him more than words can ever say. He showed me that even in a world full of judgment, there is room for a love that doesn't make sense to others but makes all the difference to the one who experiences it.

This wasn't a story of forever, but it was one of healing. In the midst of confusion and failure, he gave me clarity and strength. I don't condone what we did, but I understand why it mattered to me. And sometimes, that's enough.

**

As I reflect on my first love—and my first heartbreak—I can't help but notice a recurring pattern. The men who left the deepest imprint on me weren't the loudest or the most charismatic. They were the calm in my chaos, the quiet thinkers with steady hands and steady hearts. They were deeply grounded, emotionally intelligent, humble, and introspective—men who didn't need to raise their voices to be heard.

It's almost therapeutic, being around people like that. There's something healing about the kind of man who listens more than he speaks, who moves through the world with grace and inner strength. These were the men who knew how to slow my racing thoughts, who could balance my fire with their cool. I realize now that I've always been drawn to that type of energy; not because it completes me, but because it gives me space to breathe.

I've always been drawn to men who make space for me to be fully myself; who offer a kind of steady, nurturing love that expects nothing in return. The kind of love that feels safe, patient, and unconditional. It's not just about being cared for, but about being understood without needing to explain every part of who I am.

14: The Call I didn't Answer

My early adult years—my early twenties—were, in a way, steady. Or at least, steady in the kind of way that made sense to me. I wasn't chasing after some grand narrative or trying to live a wildly extravagant life. I dated men, broke up with them, had heartbreaks, made memories with friends, worked, moved cities, kept myself afloat. My life felt... ordinary. Manageable. And for a girl who came from chaos, that kind of ordinary felt like peace.

I went to college in South Florida. The sun, the palm trees, the humid air—it all felt like an entirely different world from the childhood I had known in upstate New York. Life there moved differently. It was louder, warmer, and somehow more forgiving. For the first time in a long time, I felt free.

**

And let's talk about being a college student.

It was wild. My friend's and I would go clubbing until the crack of dawn, sweat clinging to our skin in the heavy night air. I lived for those moments, when the music was so loud it drowned out every worry.

My friends from New York would fly down any chance they got. We'd cram into my tiny apartment like sardines, tossing our bags in corners, claiming floors and couches like it was some kind of sleepover revival. When space ran out, we'd crash at friends' places—whoever had an open couch, a spare mattress, or even just a clean bit of carpet. We didn't care. What mattered was that we were together.

We lived at the beach like it was our personal church. Every free hour was spent soaking up the sun, sand sticking to our skin, salt in our hair, laughing so hard it hurt. We'd bring snacks, speakers, and just enough sunscreen to feel responsible, but mostly, we just brought ourselves. Some of the best conversations of my life happened under those Florida skies, laying on beach towels, watching the tide come in.

It was chaotic, a little reckless, and beautifully free. There was no pressure to be anything other than exactly who we were in those moments: young, alive, and chasing the kind of happiness that didn't ask for permission.

**

And I was hustling hard. I worked three jobs to keep myself afloat. During the day, I was a nanny. When I wasn't nannying, I was a paralegal at a law firm, trying to stay tethered to the dream I had of one day becoming a lawyer. And at night, I transformed into a bottle girl at a nightclub in Miami—heels, short skirts, VIP booths, and pouring overpriced champagne for people who would never remember my name. It was chaos. It was exhausting. But I had the energy back then. I had that unstoppable 20-something grit.

I've never been someone who fits neatly into a single category. My interests have always spanned across different worlds, and college was the perfect reflection of that. I juggled multiple roles. In between all that, I was also a proud member of my school's chess league. One minute, I'd be in heels serving champagne in a crowded club, and the next, I'd be deep in thought across a chessboard in a silent auditorium. I've always moved fluidly between worlds, never settling into just one identity—and honestly, I like it that way.

Looking back, it was one of the best chapters of my life. I lived hard and loved harder. I laughed more than I cried, and for the first time in years, I felt like I was writing a story that belonged to me—not one shaped by trauma or survival, but one shaped by choice. It was a good time to be alive.

But eventually, I felt that pull again; that quiet whisper that told me I was meant for something more. So, I packed up and decided to head back up north for law school. I told myself this time would be different, that this was finally the path I was meant to be on. Spoiler: I never became a lawyer. Almost. There's that word again—*almost*—trailing behind me like a shadow I can never quite shake.

**

Overall, life in my twenties were steady. I had jobs that paid well, a routine that made sense, and a version of stability that, for once, didn't feel like it was about to collapse. Those years were the most grounded I had ever been. Chaos wasn't chasing me. I wasn't constantly looking over my shoulder or questioning if everything was going to fall apart. For the first time in a long time, I felt like I was standing on solid ground—not sand, not broken glass, but actual, steady ground. I was showing up to work. I had benefits. I had structure. I had my own place and control over my life.

I traveled often. Whenever I could, really. I hopped on flights with little hesitation, chasing new places, new energy, and brief escapes. There was something about being in motion that soothed me. Airports felt like liminal spaces where nothing was required of me except movement. I collected memories in different cities, took photos I never posted, and shared belly-aching laughter with friends who made life feel light.

There were nights where we stayed up too late, wine glasses half-full, trading stories that veered from ridiculous to raw without warning. I felt free during those years. Not wildly free, but peacefully free. I wasn't searching for perfection—I was just living in a way that felt right for me. My life wasn't extraordinary in the way some people chase Instagram-worthy moments, but it was real, it was mine, and it was good. I was content. I didn't need constant excitement. I just needed calm, connection, and authenticity. And for a while, I had that. And it meant everything.

For someone like me, who had spent so much of life surviving storm after storm, that kind of calm was everything. I was the most stable version of myself. The version I had always hoped I'd be one day.

**

My twenties were filled with quiet moments of triumph and equally quiet moments of breakdown. I wasn't always graceful. I wasn't always sure of myself. But I never stopped moving. I was proud of the woman I was becoming, even if I didn't always recognize her in the mirror. And in those years—those seemingly steady, predictable, in-between years—I found pieces of myself I didn't know I had lost. I learned that normalcy, however fleeting, is a gift. That peace, even if temporary, is worth holding onto. That growth doesn't always look like progress. Sometimes, it looks like staying still long enough to catch your breath.

But as life would later remind me, stability doesn't mean immunity from heartbreak or loss. It just means the fall hits a little harder when you thought you'd finally figured it all out. I didn't know then that the ground beneath me would eventually shift in a way I wasn't prepared for. That grief would come knocking in a way I couldn't ignore. But for a while, I had peace.

**

In 2019, that quiet kind of stability and peace collapsed—and it collapsed in the cruelest way. Up until that point, my early adult years had been steady in a way that made sense to me. I had experienced heartache and disappointment before, sure, but I managed. I coped. I had found rhythm in my routines, a life of dating, working, laughing, crying, growing. I thought I was okay. But 2019... it unraveled me in ways I'm still piecing together.

In 2019, I lost someone. Not just someone—I lost a friend. A soul-deep, irreplaceable kind of friend. The kind of friend you don't make twice in a lifetime. And even now, with all this time and pain between then and now, I hesitate to write her name. Not out of shame or discomfort, but out of respect. Out of tenderness. Out of fear, maybe.

Because her name carries weight. It holds laughter, secrets, years of trust. It holds memories that are mine, and memories that belong to her family too. And if her mother—who loved her more than anything—were to stumble upon these words, I don't know if it would bring her comfort or reopen wounds that have barely scarred over. That thought alone makes my fingers pause every time I get to her name.

I carry her name in silence. Not because I want to hide her, but because I want to protect what we had. And maybe, in some quiet, sacred way, that's how I keep her alive.

This silence, this hesitation... it's not because she isn't worth speaking about—she is worth everything. It's because her death isn't a story I ever wanted to tell. Because naming her makes it real again. And real hurts.

**

We met as camp counselors the summer of my sophomore year in high school. From the moment we talked, there was something about her, this innate warmth. She was one of the few people who truly knew me. We didn't live in the same state for most of our friendship. She was in New York, I was in Florida then Massachusetts, then Pennsylvania, then Delaware, then Illinois—but the distance never mattered. She was like a secret diary I could call. I could tell her things I never told anyone else, and she never judged me. Not once.

Ours was the kind of friendship that didn't require daily communication. We could go months without speaking and then, on a random Thursday, pick up right where we left off. No awkwardness, no explanation. Just two hearts always in sync.

Then came that night in 2019.

**

I was in Chicago then, stressed. I was trying to get through a major exam for work. My mom and two nieces were visiting from New York the following week, and I just wanted to get everything out of the way so I could enjoy their visit. That's all I was focused on—passing that exam and being present with my family.

She called me twice. Around 10 p.m.
And I didn't answer.

I didn't even hesitate to ignore the call. I saw her name flash across the screen and thought, *"I'll call her back tomorrow."* I thought it was just a random check-in, or maybe she needed to vent about something. I told myself I'd talk to her once the exam was done. I didn't know it would be the last time she'd ever call me.

The next morning, her mother called me. She was crying.

Her voice shook as she said, *"She's gone."*

Gone.
Just like that.

She had been killed by her boyfriend.
Murder-suicide.

My world shattered.

**

There's no poetic way to say it. No calm, wise metaphor that wraps the pain in a pretty bow. It just broke. Violently. Silently. Irreversibly.

I remember sitting there, phone in hand, staring at the screen like it would give me answers. The missed calls were right there. Those fucking missed calls. And I missed it. I missed her. And whatever I could've said, whatever she might've needed in that moment, it vanished into the kind of silence that never ends. It just keeps ringing in my head like an alarm I can't shut off.

I've replayed that night in my head more times than I can count. It's like a horror loop, a sick little mental game I can't seem to pause. I go back to the moment before the first call. What was I doing? Why didn't I answer? Why didn't I feel that something was wrong? Why the hell didn't I just pick up?

I hated myself for it then, and if I'm being honest, I still do.

The guilt isn't cinematic. It doesn't fade with time or grow quiet. It's loud. It gnaws. It's a shadow that never leaves the corner of my eye. Every time I hear a phone ring unexpectedly from those I love, my stomach flips. Every time I see her name in old messages, the air leaves my lungs all over again.

People talk about grief like it's a process—like it has steps and closure. But no one talks about the kind of grief that stays messy. The kind that festers. The kind that drags itself into every room you walk into. That's what this is. It's not just sadness, it's fury. It's regret. It's a scream locked inside my ribcage that never gets out.

I missed those calls. And some days, it feels like I missed my last chance to be there for her. That kind of thing? It brands you. Forever.

**

For days, I didn't cry. I didn't talk. I didn't feel. I dissociated. I went to work on no sleep. I moved through the world like a robot—silent, numb, hollow. I told no one. Not a coworker, not a friend. I kept it tucked deep in my chest like a wound I didn't deserve to show. And no one noticed.

No one but my mom.

When she arrived in Chicago, she knew immediately. She knew and said, *"What's wrong?"* I brushed it off, but she knew something was off about me. So I told her, in the softest voice possible, *"I lost a friend."* That was all I said.

I didn't tell her how deep the guilt ran. I didn't tell her about the missed call. I didn't tell her how I was screaming inside. I smiled, spent time with my nieces, played the part of the good daughter for the rest of their visit. But once they left, I crumbled again. The dissociation returned. I withdrew into the quiet shell I had known all too well growing up.

You see…I've known death. I've known pain. I've watched people I love pass, and I've managed to hold it together each time. It never broke me. Until this.

This death did something different.

I eventually sought therapy. I started writing again in my journal. I poured myself into these pages. I tried to be honest with myself. I tried to forgive myself. And still, on nights when the world feels a little too still, I wonder what could've been different had I just picked up the phone.

**

That year—2019—broke me. I had always been cracked—held together by hope, routine, maybe even denial—but 2019 shattered whatever pieces were left. It didn't just break me; it confirmed what I had feared all along—that I was already broken, and that year just made it official.

There was no putting things back the way they were. No pretending I was whole. 2019 didn't just add more scars to my already scarred body and mind, it tore open old wounds I thought had healed, then carved new ones right on top. It didn't ask for permission. It didn't give me space to breathe. It came like a storm I couldn't outrun, wrecking everything fragile I had managed to piece together. By the time the year ended, I wasn't just wounded, I was gutted. Left with nothing but silence, grief, and the weight of memories that refused to let go.

**

And because I was broken, I went on to break something else: a relationship that might've turned into something real. He was kind. Steady. Patient. A good man for me. And I wasn't ready. I was volatile. Emotionally spiraling. I pushed him away.

I lied to him. I held back parts of myself, buried the ugliest truths, sugarcoated the broken edges. I kept secrets—not because I wanted to manipulate—but because I was terrified. Terrified of what he'd think if he saw the full picture. The real me. The me that was still bleeding inside from a death I hadn't even begun to process. The me that was carrying years of emotional rot from a childhood I wouldn't wish on anyone.

He didn't trust me. And why should he? Lies, no matter how small or "protective," corrode the foundation of something real. We fought. Often. And beneath the surface of those arguments was this unspoken truth: I wasn't showing up as my full self. I was hiding in plain sight.

What I should've done was just sit him down and say: *I'm fucked up. Mentally. Emotionally. I'm not okay. I don't know how to be okay. I'm still grieving someone I loved deeply, and that grief is messy and raw and sometimes it makes me shut down. I dissociate. I disappear. I shut people out. I panic. I sabotage.* But how do you tell that to someone who just walked into your life and seems like everything good and pure? How do you drop that on someone barely two weeks in?

So instead, I did what trauma taught me: I kept quiet. I withheld. I gave half-truths, masked pain with sarcasm, distanced myself whenever things felt too close. I told myself I was protecting him—but really, I was just too afraid of being rejected for who I really was.

And that came with a price. I lost him.

I lost someone who didn't deserve to carry the weight of my silence. He walked away—not because he was cruel— but because I didn't give him the chance to stay for the real me. Not the filtered, guarded, edited version I presented. But the raw, cracked, grieving version. The one still trying to figure out how to love without running. The one still learning how to let someone love her back.

I told myself I'd never make that mistake again. But some damage sticks with you. And some people? You don't just lose them. You carry that loss forever.

**

Sometimes I wonder, if she hadn't died, would I have been better? Would I have been whole enough to let love in? Would I be married by now, living a completely different life?

I don't know.

And maybe I'll never know.

But what I do know is that grief lingers in strange ways. It latches onto the ordinary—like a phone call, an exam, a missed opportunity—and makes them monumental. It turns small choices into lifelong regrets. And yet, somehow, we keep going. We find a way to carry both the pain and the healing.

She's still with me. In every moment I question my worth. In every time I stop writing and think, *"Would she be proud of this?"* I carry her memory, not just as a ghost of what I lost, but as a reminder of what love looks like when it's honest and unwavering.

15: The Spiral and the Spark

2020.

The year the world broke. But in a sick way, it was the year I began to feel whole again. While people were screaming about empty grocery shelves, fear of touching doorknobs, and arguments over masks—I was thriving in the silence. I needed isolation more than I needed people. The world forced everyone to hide, and for once, I didn't feel weird for doing the same.

For the rest of the world, it was chaos. For me, it was peace. I finally had a reason to be alone. The isolation that suffocated others was a blanket for me. It wrapped me up and let me scream in private. I didn't have to pretend anymore. I could cry into pillows, scream into silence, write every dark thought down in my journal and not worry about how insane I looked. No one was watching. The world was hiding, and I was grateful.

I didn't isolate to meditate or become spiritually enlightened. No. I isolated to scream. Into my pillow. Into my journal. Into nothing. I screamed in silence where no one could witness how close to the edge I really was. I started working out again. Journaling. Crying when I needed to. I started healing. Not in the traditional, beautiful Instagram-worthy way, but in a raw, messy, screaming-into-nothingness kind of way. And for the first time since my friend's death, I felt strong. Stronger than before. I loved the lockdown. It gave me myself back. Everyone was watching CNN or death counters. I was watching the clock between journal entries and workout routines.

I loved the COVID lockdown. I didn't speak to anyone about how I still hated myself for that missed phone call in 2019. I didn't share my grief. I wore a mask long before COVID made it mandatory. But for once, I could cry in the dark without having to clean up my face before facing the world. There was no world to face.

By the time 2021 rolled around, I was doing better. I was living again. Smiling for real. Hopeful. I somehow thought I found peace.

But like anything in my life, nothing good stays for long.

**

Late 2021 came around like it had something to prove. I should've known better than to trust peace. One group chat message in November detonated whatever fragile stability I had. It was about him—my twin in another form. My friend. The messages were from family members of someone who had meant the world to me—someone whose story is not mine to tell in full, but whose presence in my life shaped me deeply. We shared a kindred history of abandonment, trauma, survival. Except while I drowned in emotions, he channeled his into greatness. He became an incredible athlete. I admired everything about him.

The group chat was a plea. A cry for help. He was having panic attacks, seizures. People were worried. I dropped everything and flew to be with him. Because he had always been my number one supporter through everything in life. We walked the town, talked like we always did. There's this moment that still sticks with me—we passed by this wall with graffiti that read: *"Crawl, walk, run. But whatever you do, keep moving forward."* I smiled and asked why I'd never noticed it before.

He said, "Sometimes you gotta look where no one's looking to find the dope shit."

**

A month later, his name was on the news. I don't need to say it. The grief still haunts me in a quiet way. And if that wasn't enough, two months later, my dog—my sweet girl of 18 years— passed away. Her name was Zi. She was my soul dog. My shadow. My constant. Losing her didn't just feel like losing a pet—it was like losing the last living part of my younger self. And it was too much. And just like that, I lost two lifelines in a matter of weeks.

People say "it's just a dog," but to me? She was family. Therapy wasn't an option—I'd taken a risky job at a startup that paid less, and money was tight. I couldn't afford the help I desperately needed.

I shut down. I spiraled. Hard.

I slept for days. I stopped eating. I didn't shower. The only thing that forced me out of bed was my other dog needing to be let out. Otherwise, I buried myself under sheets like they could protect me from the noise in my head.

I had left a long-term, secure job earlier that year for a flashy tech startup. Everyone around me said it was the move. "Ground floor," they said. "Innovative." "You'll get in early—ride the wave." I believed them. I wanted to believe them. I had been with my previous company for seven years, and while it was safe, it was also draining in ways I couldn't articulate. I thought this new startup would be a fresh beginning—something that could ignite the spark again.

It paid less, but I justified it to myself as a tradeoff. I was one of the first people hired. I helped build systems and processes from the ground up. I was working directly with the founders. In my mind, I believed I could grow into something big. Maybe even land a leadership position. Maybe even get equity. That word—*equity*—held so much promise. But dreams like that always come with a cost. And mine came at the price of stability. I cut my salary almost in half, thinking I could "make it work." But the reality hit quickly: I couldn't afford therapy. Not even close.

And I needed therapy.

I was unraveling slowly, methodically, every day a little number, a little more disconnected, and a little more lost. The weight of grief, unresolved trauma, and silence pressed on me like a slow suffocation. But instead of therapy, instead of structured help, what I got were friends—unexpected, unrelenting, beautiful friends—who saved me in ways they never knew.

**

Candace, Jess, Shar, Marcus. They showed up. Physically, emotionally. They didn't ask what was wrong. They didn't demand answers. They just came. They forced me out of my house when I didn't want to leave. Made me walk when I wanted to lie down. Gave me food when I hadn't eaten. Made me laugh when all I wanted to do was scream.

While I had friends who showed up in person—who hugged me, walked beside me, got me out of the house—there was one friend who supported me from behind a screen. Blaise. He's been my quiet, steady support system for years. A digital lifeline. We went to high school together. He never asked for anything, never demanded my attention. He just… showed up. Quietly. Reliably. Kindly.

He understood the shape of my depression in a way most people couldn't. He never pushed me to talk when I wasn't ready. He never got upset when I didn't respond for months at a time. His messages would come like clockwork—gentle check-ins, thoughtful little nudges reminding me that someone out there hadn't forgotten I existed. And when I finally did respond, even after months of silence, he never guilted me. Never questioned me. Just welcomed me back with warmth and understanding.

In a world where I often felt like I was failing everyone, where every unread message added to my shame, my friends reminded me what grace looked like. Their presence, even in small doses, let me breathe in moments I was drowning. They reminded me that connection doesn't always have to be loud or constant to be meaningful. It just has to be real. They didn't heal me, not completely. But they slowed the freefall. They helped me breathe again. In their own way, they became the therapy I couldn't afford. The medicine I didn't know how to ask for.

Without knowing it, they pulled me back from the edge. And for that, I owe them everything.

**

But during those years, every time I tried to pull myself out a dark hole, the darkness swallowed me whole again. I sank right back into that familiar black pit, spiraling deeper than before.

I quit the tech startup job not long after in early 2022. I told people it was because I needed a change, but the truth is—I couldn't keep pretending. I couldn't fake enthusiasm for some AI platform or SaaS bullshit when I couldn't even fake wanting to wake up in the morning. I was dying inside and logging into Zoom meetings acting like I cared about customer engagement metrics. I didn't. I barely cared if I ate that day.

I jumped into another job, hoping maybe a new environment would fix what was broken. Spoiler: it didn't. That job was far worse. It was the kind of place where burnout wasn't just accepted—it was expected. The tools were outdated, and one of my managers? A toxic power-tripping nightmare who talked to people like they were beneath him.

As part of my job, I was required to read and discuss books that had no direct connection to my actual work responsibilities. I found this odd, especially in the industry I was in, finances, auditing, compliance, investments. While I understand the intent may have been team-building or professional development, the activity felt more like a social book club than a meaningful part of my role. Since everything was so manual and there was no relevant training for the actual context of my work, spending an hour each day discussing a book unrelated to my role felt like a poor use of time and resources.

Ultimately, I found that the position did not align with my professional goals or expectations. Eventually, I stopped trying to care about the job; I just had no passion for the work I was doing. I love writing and I love reading, but when you're burned out from the day and then expected to read a mandatory book that has nothing to do with your actual role, it starts to feel like work never ends. I'd log off for the day, only to pick up the book my manager assigned, and honestly, it felt more like being back in high school than being a professional. It got frustrating. I lasted six months.

They fired me.

And I didn't blink. I smiled.

No tears. No panic. No shame. Just a numb sort of freedom. I wasn't even sad. I was relieved. That job was soul rot. Good riddance.

**

So here I was…my bank account was low. My energy was lower. My self-worth was nonexistent. The depression didn't just creep in anymore—it lived with me, made itself at home, took over my bed, my fridge, my future. I wasn't living. I was waiting for something—anything—to make me feel again.

But nothing did.

The worst part wasn't the job loss. I've survived worse. The worst part was me—what I'd become. I ghosted everyone. Not out of cruelty. Not even out of apathy. Just... survival. I couldn't keep up the act anymore. I didn't want to show people the walking corpse I'd become.

The weight gain made me hide more. I felt disgusting in my own skin—like a stranger wearing a costume made of shame. Every inch I put on felt like punishment. I hated the way my clothes fit, the way mirrors looked at me, the way I looked back. I wanted to disappear into the floor, melt into the shadows. And some nights… I wished I would just vanish. Just stop existing altogether.

My remaining dog, my last constant; the only living being I could stand to be around—Petey—kept me tethered to this life. Barely. He tried to keep me alive the only way he knew how. Every morning, he'd gently rest his head on the edge of my bed, his soft tongue brushing against my face, nudging me out of the dark. It wasn't just affection. It was survival. He was reminding me: "You're still here. Get up."

He was happy, innocent, full of life and wonder. The polar opposite of me. He greeted every walk like it was a gift, every meal like it was a feast, every moment like it mattered. I envied that about him. I envied the purity of it. I felt like a monster beside him. I was bitter, withdrawn, hollowed out from the inside, and held together by routine. But he didn't care. He loved me anyway. No conditions. No expectations. Just love. Just presence.

Still, I felt disgusting. Useless. Dead inside. I didn't want to see people. I didn't want people to see me. I ghosted the world. Deleted apps. Stopped posting on social media. Stopped replying. I didn't check social media for months—sometimes I forgot it even existed. My world had shrunk down to two things: me and my dog. My four walls, and the sound of his paws following me from room to room.

**

2022 to early 2024 was a mess. A shitshow I don't even like to replay in my mind. I was a ghost in my own life—drifting, watching everything around me move while I stayed frozen. There were days I didn't talk to a single soul. I'd sit in silence until the sun went down, and then sit in more silence as the night took over. I'd eat mindlessly, scroll randomly, sleep endlessly. Or not at all.

Sometimes I think maybe it's a blessing that no one saw that version of me. That I never let the outside world in. That I never had to explain how deeply broken I felt. Because if they had seen it, I don't think they would have recognized me.

In early 2024, something inside me cracked. Or maybe it had been cracking for a long time and I just finally heard it break. It was 4 a.m. and I was wide awake—again. My eyes burned from hours of scrolling, job forums open on every tab, résumés blurred into a sea of generic applications. I wasn't just looking for work. I was searching for a way out. A way out of this version of myself I couldn't stand anymore.

I was looking for an escape. From the mess I had become. From the loneliness. From the rot. I applied to anything that sounded remotely tolerable. Marketing coordinator, project assistant, customer success manager—whatever so as long as it was a remote position. Because I didn't want anyone to see the mess I was. It didn't matter what it was, I just needed something to shake me out of the numbness. I needed something to feel *real* again.

But the truth? I didn't want another job. I wanted to disappear. I wanted to unplug from the life I was stuck in and vanish into something entirely different. I was searching for something I couldn't even name. Not purpose. Not meaning. Just... something. A crack of light. A reason to keep moving.

I was searching for a life that didn't require me to show up at a physical office every day. More than just a preference, it was a deep need to escape. The corporate world was draining me—mentally, emotionally, and even physically. The rigid structure, the endless meetings, the performative productivity...it all left me feeling trapped and disconnected from any real sense of purpose. I wasn't just burned out; I was suffocating in a system that didn't align with who I was or who I wanted to become. I craved freedom, creativity, and space to breathe; things the corporate grind rarely offers.

In the job I had at the time, I didn't feel like I was bringing much value—especially after they hired another employee with more experience than me. It wasn't that I didn't know my stuff; I did. But I often felt overshadowed. My colleague had a stronger, more assertive presence, and that made me hesitant to speak up or share my ideas. I started to shrink back, not because I lacked knowledge, but because I felt outmatched by his confidence. That silence began to impact my performance, and deep down, I knew it was only a matter of time before I'd be let go. Strangely, that thought didn't scare me. If anything, it felt like I was quietly hoping for it, because I was ready for something new. I needed a reset. A new life.

And in that restless, sleep-deprived haze—eyes bloodshot, heart racing but soul numb—something deep inside whispered: *You've clawed your way through hell for years. For what? What would the version of you ten years from now say, looking back at this exact moment? Would she beg you to stop just surviving? Would she scream at you to stop waiting for the right time to be happy, to finally live your life like it actually belongs to you? Would she be angry you kept putting your joy on hold for another day that might never come? Or would she plead with you to choose yourself—right now—while there's still something left to save?*

That's when I stopped scrolling through job boards and endless listings. I paused and asked myself a deeper question: what do I actually enjoy? What kind of work would allow me to wake up each morning feeling excited, fulfilled—even happy—to start the day? I realized I had been chasing jobs out of necessity, not passion. So instead of asking, *what can I get hired for*, I started asking…*what kind of life do I want to build?*

Ideas started to form.

Maybe it was the fact that I'd spent two years in hiding. Maybe it was the job boards that all looked the same. Or maybe it was a sleepless night where I finally snapped and asked myself, *"Is this it? Is this how you want your story to end? Almost?"* And out of nowhere, one voice in my head whispered: *Start your own business.*

I wrote down random ideas. Pages of them. And then one stuck. It was wild. It was stupid. It was desperate. But it felt like me. I spent two hours drafting a business plan. I sent it to a friend who I considered a mentor. He read it and responded a week later, "It's random. It's crazy. But sometimes madness is what you need to light a fire. Tia I am proud of you. Go for it."

I didn't just send my business idea to one person—I also told *her*. Sonya. My second mother. The one who had seen me at my lowest, year after year. She had known the full weight of my depression—hell, she carried it with me more times than I can count. And truthfully, I hated that. I hated that every time she heard from me, it was darkness. Always a crisis. Always pain. Maybe sending her my business plan wasn't just about sharing news—it was about proving to her, and to myself, that I wasn't just this fucked-up, broken thing. That there was still a version of me worth rooting for.

And like she always does, she showed up. No hesitation. No fluff. Just real, pure, unfiltered support. She replied with joy that felt like a lifeline. It wasn't performative. It wasn't polite. It was *real*. That's what Sonya is—real. A soul-saver in disguise. She'll never fully understand what she's meant to me over the years. But there's a reason I call her my second mother—and it's not just out of affection. It's survival. Without her, there are parts of me that would've stayed buried.

**

I started my business on a random Tuesday, born out of sleep deprivation, heartbreak, and sheer desperation. That business was born not from ambition, but from desperation. It was a lifeline. A rope thrown to a woman drowning in her own grief. But sometimes, rock bottom gives you the clearest view of the sky. And now? I'm climbing again.

PHASE 4: Return
Integration, lost and found, purpose, peace

16: Letters to Nowhere, Messages from Everywhere

In early 2021, after a year of clawing my way out of the darkness; after spending 2020 rebuilding the pieces of myself that hadn't already crumbled from my friend's death in 2019, I was finally starting to feel like I had some semblance of peace. I was eating better. I was working out. I was keeping myself afloat. But peace is dangerous when you've lived in chaos most of your life. Stillness makes room for the ghosts to creep in.

One night, in the quiet hours where sleep never came, I found myself going down the kind of rabbit hole only the internet can offer. No plan, no direction, just that aching curiosity that lives in the gut of every adopted kid: Who am I, really? I opened up my laptop, numb, and started searching for anything—something.

I logged into my 23andMe account. I had joined back in 2018 when I thought maybe, just maybe, the world had a sliver of magic left in it. But over the years, the matches were disappointing at best. Most were so far removed—0.0000000001% related. Useless, laughable. Strangers with almost no ties to me in their data pool. I never held out real hope. My family—if you could even call it that—was from a rural, impoverished part of Vietnam. I remembered growing up with no electricity, no plumbing, no doors that locked. We didn't have toilets—we dug holes in the dirt and called it a bathroom. We were poor. I'm talking dirt poor. The kind of poverty that leaves permanent scars on your body and your mind. And I knew that no one from my bloodline was paying $99 for a DNA test, let alone knew what 23andMe even was.

So, I told myself the truth: I wasn't going to find them there. Not really.

But then something in me whispered, Try Facebook. I figured; I know where I was born. Maybe someone from that town, someone with my last name, might exist online. Maybe they said something, posted something. Maybe I'd see a face that looked like mine.

It was years since I had last logged on Facebook. I didn't check my messages. I avoided it like the plague. But something told me to open my inbox. Something told me to scroll. That's when I saw it—a message. One I had never opened. It was from someone who claimed they were from the same orphanage as me.

And just like that, everything shifted. That single line: *"We were in the same orphanage"*. It wasn't proof. It wasn't a parent. It wasn't a reunion. But it was something. Something real. Something from my past I didn't have to beg to remember.

**

The message came from a girl who said she was from the same orphanage as me. She said she was trying to reconnect all the children who had once lived there. My first instinct? Delete. Walk away. Bury it. Why would I willingly rip open a wound that had never really healed? My past in Vietnam wasn't a warm, nostalgic thing—it was full of trauma, gaps, silence. Reaching back into that would've been like digging my own grave, not knowing if I could crawl back out.

But curiosity is a strange thing. No matter how much hurt is tied to the past, the question of who you are—where you came from—never really leaves you. It lingers like a ghost in the room. I grew up watching my friends laugh about how they had their mom's nose or their dad's eyes. I had no one to compare myself to. No one to say, "You have your uncle's laugh," or "That's your grandmother's stubbornness." That kind of curiosity doesn't go away. It just burrows deeper over time.

My adoptive parents and I tried. For years, we sent letters to the adoption agency that once handled my case, clinging to hope that someone—anyone—on the other end would respond. But there was only silence. No updates. No forwarding information.

When I became an adult, I took matters into my own hands. I reached out directly to the agency, hoping that maybe, as an adult, I'd be granted access to the answers I'd been denied. But again—nothing. It was like screaming into a void, like our letters and pleas disappeared into the air, unanswered and unseen. The silence was frustrating.

I remember being so desperate that I took a friend's advice of submitting my story to a popular Vietnamese television show known for heartwarming reunions—stories of long-lost family members finding each other again, joyful tear-filled moments caught on camera. I thought maybe, someone would read my message and want to help. But no response ever came.

Late at night, when sleep escaped me, I'd sit at my computer, endlessly scrolling the internet, searching for anything that resembled my hometown—images, names, old landmarks—anything that might feel familiar. I joined forums and message boards, typing out fragmented memories and vague descriptions, hoping a stranger might recognize something. I posted blindly, reaching out into the void. But each time, I was met with silence. Nothing came of it. Just more unanswered calls into a space where I felt invisible.

You'd think in a world obsessed with heartwarming stories of reunion, in a society that celebrates family reconnections on talk shows and viral videos, there would be more empathy built into these systems. More humanity. But what I experienced instead was bureaucracy. Cold policies. Missing records. Closed doors.

And that's what people don't understand about adoption—it doesn't always come with a tidy ending or a perfectly timed reunion. Sometimes it comes with years of silence, with rejection, with wondering whether anyone on the other side is even trying to remember you.

And yet, one click—only one click—on a Facebook message opened a door I had been pounding on my whole life.

**

That one message introduced me to people from the orphanage. People who remembered me. People who raised me. And suddenly, like floodgates bursting, information came pouring in—names, details, pieces of a puzzle I had spent decades chasing. It was almost laughable how easy it was the information came to me. After all those unanswered letters, all those ignored emails, all the hopeless nights of wondering if I was just a ghost to the world—I finally got answers.

And it messed me up. Because how could one message solve what years of effort couldn't? It made me question everything. Was it all some twisted form of control from the orphanage, some buried corruption from the government to keep this information from us? Or maybe the orphanage really thought they were protecting us—protecting me—by keeping quiet, not responding to emails and letters. Maybe they thought the truth would hurt more than the silence.

But honestly? I don't know. And maybe it's better that I don't. Some answers come with more pain than peace.

**

Through this group, I found them—my blood. My family. I found my grandmother—still alive. I found my sister. I found my aunt and uncle—the ones who once pushed for me to be given away. It all came crashing down on me so fast I could barely keep up. Joy collided with anger. Confusion mixed with grief. I was overwhelmed with feelings I hadn't prepared for. I was happy but broken. I was grateful but hurt. I was shocked but hollow.

The first time I video-called them, it didn't feel real. The screen lit up with faces that I couldn't seem to recognize. It was like watching a dream that didn't belong to me. I cried, not because I knew exactly what I was feeling—but because I didn't. It was everything and nothing all at once. I wanted to fly back to Vietnam right then—2021—but I couldn't. They didn't know it, but I was still in survival mode, fighting demons that had nothing to do with them. I was clawing my way out of years of trauma, heartbreak, and unresolved grief. They were a piece of my story, but I had to deal with my American life—the part they never saw.

So, I postponed it. I told myself I'd go the following year—sometimes at the end of 2022. But life had other plans for me.

**

Between losing a friend and then my dog within weeks of each other in late 2021, my world already felt like it was falling apart. Then, in early 2022, I received word from my family in Vietnam that my grandmother's health was rapidly declining. I hadn't seen her in nearly 30 years. The urgency in their voices struck a chord in me. There was no time to think. The clock was ticking. Something in me knew that if I didn't go now, I'd regret it for the rest of my life. I wasn't ready emotionally, mentally—hell, I could barely get out of bed most days—but I booked the ticket anyway.

But when I arrived in the village, something didn't sit right. My grandmother, the woman I was told was fading fast, greeted me with the strength and energy of someone far from fragile. She was walking, talking just fine. I was stunned. A part of me couldn't help but wonder if my family had used her health as a way to bait me—believing that this was the only thing powerful enough to get me to come home.

And maybe they were right. Maybe I needed that kind of push. Because as much as I was caught off guard by the truth, I don't regret going. Seeing her again was healing in a way I never anticipated. It was chaotic, confusing, and emotionally raw—but it reminded me that closure doesn't always come in neat packages. Sometimes, it comes in the form of imperfect reunions and complicated truths.

**

Part of me also hoped that Vietnam would offer the healing I couldn't find in America. A new environment, a break from the weight I carried every day. Maybe facing the past would help fix the present. Or maybe I just wanted to run. Either way, two weeks later, I was on a plane leaving Chicago. Destination: Hanoi.

17: Closure in the Dust

If you ask me what fear is, I'd say this: fear isn't always screaming or running away. Sometimes, fear is the quiet voice in your head convincing you not to try. It's the ache in your chest when you're about to make a life-altering decision. It's the paralysis before boarding a flight to a country you haven't seen in 30 years.

It shows up in different forms—when you're sitting in a remote village, unsure of who to trust, or when you look into the eyes of a stranger and wonder if your life is in danger. But fear also hides in places you least expect it—in the fear of being forgotten, unloved, misunderstood, or left behind.

And yet, I've learned that fear is not the enemy. It's a signal. It tells you that something matters deeply. That you're stepping into something real. That there's risk, but also possibility. Fear can be the hand that holds you back or the fire that pushes you forward. Most of my life, I've chosen the latter.

You see…I've never been someone who fears much. If I'm being honest, I'm probably too fearless for my own good. It's a trait that has served me well in some moments…and put me in danger in others.

I do 98% of my traveling alone. Most of what I experience in this life, I go through on my own. I gravitate toward places others avoid…the hidden alleys, the unfamiliar towns, the parts of the world that don't show up in travel guides. There's something about the unknown that pulls me in.

So, when I decided to fly to Vietnam to meet my biological family after more than 25 years of silence, it wasn't shocking to those who knew me. Still, the weight of that decision was heavier than most. I was heading into rural Bắc Giang, deep in the countryside, where internet connection was spotty at best, and the reality of human trafficking and drug trafficking in Southeast Asia still lingers like an unspoken threat. Especially in the very province where I was born.

But that didn't stop me. My fearless side—maybe even the reckless side, won. I didn't have a solid plan. I didn't know what I was walking into. All I had was a name, a blurry sense of connection, and the kind of trust that doesn't make sense to most people.

People always ask how I do things like this, how I walk into the unknown without flinching. The truth is, it's not about bravery. It's about hunger. A hunger to know who I am, where I came from, and what pieces of my past I've left buried for too long.

I wasn't looking for comfort. I wasn't looking for safety. I was looking for closure. And sometimes, closure requires a bit of madness.

**

When I arrived in Song Vân, familiarity hit me fast. The air was thick with the smell of dirt and smoke, the kind that clings to your skin and makes every breath feel heavy. The roads were just as dusty and narrow as I remembered, lined with rice paddies, and scattered homes that looked like they hadn't changed in decades. It was both foreign and familiar. Like walking through a dream I forgot I had.

The countryside of Vietnam hadn't changed much. Kids still ran barefoot in the streets, elders still gathered on plastic chairs sipping tea, and the smell of rain on hot concrete still brought a kind of nostalgia I didn't know I held in me. I remembered flashes of this life. A tin bowl. A water pump. A dog barking at the edge of a dusty field. Time had passed, but here—it felt still.

Meeting my grandmother and sister in person was surreal. There was no magical reunion moment like the movies. No dramatic embrace. Just awkward smiles, long stares, and tears that didn't know whether they came from joy or pain. These were people who shared my blood, but not my life. And in that moment, I didn't feel some grand emotional epiphany. There was no dramatic breakthrough or sudden wave of clarity.

I know it might come off as cold, but one of the deepest survival skills I carried with me from my childhood in Vietnam is the ability to disconnect. It's not that I don't feel; it's that I learned early on not to show it. Trust wasn't something handed out freely where I came from. I learned to keep my guard up, to withhold parts of myself unless someone proved they loved me unconditionally. The people in front of me now—they didn't raise me. My memories of that place aren't filled with warmth or safety; they're colored by pain, fear, and survival. So when I returned, it was hard to summon love for people tied more to the trauma of my past than to the comfort of my present. Love, for me, had become something you earn with actions, not just blood or titles.

**

I stood in front of a woman I hadn't seen in nearly three decades—my grandmother. She was 99 years old. Time had pressed into her bones, curved her back, thinned her voice, but there she was. The woman who gave life to the woman who gave me life. She sat in a wooden chair by her bed, her hands resting gently on her lap like folded silk after a lifetime of labor. Her skin was weathered, the kind only years of sun and farming can sculpt. Her eyes—one completely blind, the other dim with age—could no longer see the world clearly. And yet, the moment I walked in, she reached for my hand and said my name. She couldn't see me, but she knew it was me.

Her touch was soft. Softer than I imagined for someone who had spent decades working rice fields, raising children, burying loved ones. That day, time bent itself to us. There were no long explanations, no dramatic tears. I sat on the floor beside her for what felt like hours, holding her hand, letting her trace my face with her fingertips, watching her silently cry—tears from the corner of the eye that could still make out shadows of light.

My sister was there too. A woman I once searched for but could never find. When my adoptive parents tried to locate her to adopt her alongside me, there were no records, no names, just the memory of a girl left behind. We didn't know if she had survived. And now here she was—

standing beside our grandmother, a quiet strength in the room. My sister, with her calm demeanor, soft voice, and eyes that held more stories than she'd ever dare tell aloud. She had three kids. Her first child came when she was barely more than a child herself—13, maybe 14.

And I wondered: *If I had stayed, would this have been my life too?* Would I have been a young mother, raising kids in the heat of the Vietnamese countryside, married into survival, quietly folding away my dreams?

**

The meal was already spread on the floor by the time I walked in. A low woven mat stretched across the concrete, worn from decades of shared meals and bare feet. The food sat in simple bowls—steamed rice, steamed chicken, sautéed greens, a fish stew with tamarind that filled the room with its warm, familiar tang. My sister beckoned me over without a word, patting the space beside her. I lowered myself down cross-legged, instinctively.

This felt like déjà vu. Like muscle memory I hadn't used in years suddenly waking up. Sitting on the ground, sharing food with hands and chopsticks passed across laps, no words needed—only glances and the occasional chuckle when someone spilled rice. It was all so natural, and yet so foreign, too. I had spent most of my life trying to erase this version of myself, the version that once squatted barefoot to eat dinner in a dirt-floor home.

But the truth is, I was incredibly uncomfortable sitting on the floor. After years of growing up in the West, I had become used to a different kind of comfort—chairs with back support, tables at chest height, silverware laid out neatly beside plates. My body had adapted to a lifestyle that prioritized convenience and cushioning.

Here, though, everything was different. Meals were eaten cross-legged on the ground, shared from communal dishes. The floors were hard, the seats non-existent, and the beds? They weren't beds as I knew them. Just thin mats woven from bamboo or corn husk, spread over wooden frames or concrete. No mattresses, no softness, just the rawness of a life lived without excess.

The physical discomfort mirrored the emotional dissonance I was feeling too. I was in the land I came from, yet everything felt foreign to the version of me that had grown up worlds away.

But here, back in my cousin's home, I was reminded of why the floor always felt safer. More connected. Grounded. We shared bowls. We leaned over one another. We passed soup and small bites without the need for formality. There was no performance here. Just family. I felt like a child again, not in age, but in spirit. The way my grandmother slowly fed herself with shaky hands. The way my sister quietly piled more food into my bowl, a small smile on her face. The way her kids leaned into me, curious but respectful, as if sensing that I belonged, even if they couldn't explain why.

A silence hung between us, but it wasn't awkward. It was sacred. It was the silence that comes when food is hot and bellies are empty. When the company is enough, and no conversation is needed to fill the space. I didn't have the words anyway—my Vietnamese was still nonexistent. Google Translate could only carry me so far. So, we shared the only language we had: the meal.

**

I didn't know any Vietnamese. I spoke with my family through hand gestures and Google Translate. It wasn't perfect, but it worked. We'd sit at the kitchen table passing a phone back and forth, laughing at the mistranslations that somehow made the moment feel lighter.

It was strange—finding pieces of myself in a place that was both foreign and familiar. I had spent so much of my life wondering what I'd lost. Now, I was holding it in my hands. And it was both beautiful and unbearable. Because with the reunion came regret. I regretted the years lost. I regretted not knowing my sister's laugh as a child. I regretted that I could not bring her with me into the world I was adopted into. I regretted that our lives, once so close, had unraveled into two very different stories.

But in that little house, in a quiet village far from the chaos of city life, something settled in me. No dramatic closure. Just the understanding that life had given us all what it could, in the only way it knew how.

**

I stayed at my cousin's house. It was modest—bare-boned, really.

In rural villages across Vietnam—particularly in places like Song Vân—families often live in clusters of homes or simple huts that are closely connected, sometimes even physically attached to one another, like my family's. These homes are typically shared by multiple generations, with grandparents, parents, and children all living side by side, often under one extended roof or within a small radius. You could describe it as a kind of rural commune, not in the political sense, but in the way daily life, space, and responsibilities are shared across family lines. Meals are often cooked together, children are raised collectively, and the lives of individuals are deeply intertwined with those of their relatives and neighbors. This structure fosters a strong sense of belonging, but it can also feel stifling for those who crave independence or have strained family dynamics.

My family dynamic had always been fragile, more fractured than whole. So, the communal way of life I lived in that week felt stifling, almost suffocating at times.

I slept beneath a fan that barely stirred the heavy air, offering little relief from the oppressive heat. The humidity clung to my skin like a second layer, and the stillness of the night only made it worse. Sleep was elusive—each night I found myself tossing, turning, and waking up drenched in sweat. By the end of the week, I was running on fumes.

The night sounds of the countryside in rural Vietnam are unlike anything you experience in the city. As darkness falls, the world doesn't go quiet, it changes rhythm. Crickets begin their high-pitched symphony, blending with the deep, croaky calls of frogs in the rice paddies. Occasionally, the rustling of leaves signals a small animal or lizard darting by. Far off, a cow may groan or a rooster might crow prematurely under a moonlit sky, confused by the night. The distant bark of a village dog adds a lonely echo to it all.

In many ways, it's both eerie and comforting. The sounds remind you that you're surrounded by life…untamed, unfiltered, and indifferent to human schedules. At first, it can feel overwhelming, even unsettling. But after a few nights, there's something grounding about it. The countryside doesn't pretend to be quiet; it simply offers a different kind of noise—raw, organic, and timeless.

**

The bathroom was connected to the barn, where chickens clucked, cows mooed, and pigs shuffled in the mud just feet away. Every shower was overwhelmed by the pungent mix of manure, wet earth, and smoke from nearby fires that neighbors gathered their household waste at sunset, tossing it into open flames.

The act of showering didn't offer relief. I was swarmed by insects in the bathroom, their bites relentless even as I tried to wash off the day. When I reached for the pajamas I had laid out not even five minutes into my shower, I found large insect eggs scattered across the fabric. It was unsettling. No matter how many times I bathed, I never felt truly clean. No matter how long I stood under the cold water, I never felt truly clean. The towel I was given was thin and barely absorbent, leaving me damp and sticky as I changed into clothes that clung to my skin. The heat and humidity only worsened it, creating a permanent layer of discomfort that hung over me like a second skin.

As if that wasn't enough, the insects declared full war on me at all hours of the day. The mosquitoes must have sensed I was foreign—fresh blood—and they attacked relentlessly. By the end of the week, my legs were covered in angry red bites, swollen and irritated, so severe they resembled a rash or an allergic reaction. I scratched until I bled, desperate for relief, but the jungle didn't care. I felt like I was being devoured—bit by bit, sting by sting.

The constant humidity made everything stick to my skin, and between the bites, the sweat, and the filth, I carried a permanent discomfort that week.

**

It's astonishing how quickly I had grown used to the comforts of life in America. Returning to my hometown in Vietnam—where the beds were wooden, the heat was relentless, and the simplest daily routines required effort—made me feel soft, even weak. I hated that about myself. I felt ashamed for missing things like hot showers or clean clothes, for tossing and turning on hard mattresses, for feeling utterly drained each night. But I refused to show that weakness. I didn't want anyone to see how much I was struggling, so I pushed through—imitating the way my family moved, worked, and endured. I did everything they did.

This experience highlighted the resilience of those who live without the comforts I had taken for granted. It also made me reflect on the privileges I had grown accustomed to and the strength required to live without them. While I struggled to sleep on the hard beds and cope with the heat, my family carried on with grace and endurance. Their ability to thrive in such conditions was both humbling and inspiring.

**

It was a strange feeling staying in the very house where my pain began. The same walls that echoed with my cries as a child now echoed with quiet politeness. My aunt and uncle—the ones who hit me, who encouraged for me to be given up—offered me rice and a fan to ease the stifling heat. I accepted it all with a calm that surprised even me. Not because I forgot, but because I had already let the weight of it go.

There was no confrontation. No words exchanged about what had happened. I don't think they even knew I remembered. But I did. I always will. Still, sitting on their floor, eating food they had prepared for me, I didn't feel rage. I didn't feel hate. In fact, I felt... nothing. Not emptiness, not numbness—just empty peace. The kind that comes after a long battle, when the war is over, and you no longer have the energy to carry old wounds.

I forgave them. Quietly. In my own heart. Not because they deserved it, but because I did.

Forgiveness, I've learned, is less about freeing the other person and more about unshackling yourself. I didn't want to carry their actions around any longer. I didn't want my healing to be tethered to their remorse, or lack of it. Forgiveness, in this case, was not reconciliation. It was release.

**

The rest of that week passed in a strange blur, a blend of motion and stillness, of overwhelm and clarity. My family, in their warmth and excitement, welcomed what felt like the entire village into the home. Each day, new faces appeared at the door: distant relatives, old neighbors, strangers who remembered me as a baby. They came to say hello, to see me, to bear witness to this strange reunion that felt sacred in its own way.

I felt so much, all at once. Gratitude. Love. Confusion. Discomfort. As a child, I often found crowds and constant interaction overwhelming, and even as an adult, some of that lingers. There was no space to retreat, no quiet corner to collect myself. Every time I felt the urge to step away, another visitor arrived—curious, kind, wanting to look into my face and tell me they remembered when.

The villagers—the neighbors from long ago—they remembered me. Their eyes lit up with recognition, their voices warm with stories I had no memory of. They recalled the little girl I once was, the way I used to run barefoot through the fields, the time I scraped my knee chasing after a dog, or how I used to cling to my grandmother's áo bà ba. But for me, their faces were strangers. Their familiarity only deepened my sense of disconnection. I searched their eyes, hoping for a flicker of recognition in return—something to awaken a buried memory—but there was nothing.

It's strange—almost unsettling—that the only memories I could recall from my early childhood were moments of fear: running through the rice fields to avoid beatings, hiding, surviving. They were fragments steeped in trauma. So when the neighbors shared warm recollections of me laughing, playing, being cared for—it felt disorienting. Their stories painted a different picture of my past, one I couldn't access myself. In a way, their memories were a gift…gentler, softer truths that contrasted with the darkness I carried. And yet, it was hard to trust memories that weren't my own.

I sometimes found myself questioning whether the stories the neighbors told me were genuine or just polite fabrications shaped by cultural expectations. In many traditional Asian communities, there's an unspoken rule…what happens inside the home stays inside. Appearances are everything. There's a tendency to maintain a facade of harmony and respectability, even when the reality is far from it. Smiles can mask sorrow, and silence can be more telling than truth.

I wondered if they truly remembered joyful moments, or if they were preserving an illusion for the sake of saving face. Maybe they knew more than they let on. Perhaps they were aware of the mistreatment, but tradition and social norms demanded that they look the other way—or worse, pretend it didn't happen. It's a strange feeling, being caught between two realities: the one they tell, and the one I lived.

**

I smiled. Not out of obligation, exactly, but because I didn't know what else to do. Inside, though, I was fraying a bit. I longed for just a few quiet moments, a breath to catch between the waves of affection and memory and noise.

When it became too much, I found comfort in the most unexpected place—my cousins' children and my niece. They were young, energetic, unburdened by history or expectation. With them, I didn't have to explain anything. I could sit, play, or simply listen to their stories and laughter. They gave me an excuse to step outside, to run in the rice fields or kick a ball in the yard, to become invisible for a little while without disappearing.

Those moments—simple, quiet, unstructured—were my small acts of escape. They were how I stayed grounded in a week that threatened to sweep me away. And in the presence of those children, I found an odd sense of peace. It wasn't solitude in the traditional sense, but it was enough. Enough to breathe. Enough to carry on.

**

In that week, I felt both found and lost. I belonged, and I didn't. I was one of them, and I wasn't. It was like living in a story that wasn't entirely mine, but somehow, I'd been written into the margins. The language was familiar but foreign, the faces warm but distant. There were moments of comfort; my niece's innocent laughter, the clinking of chopsticks over a shared meal, the rustling of banana leaves in the breeze that made me feel like maybe, I had come home.

But then there were the silences too. The quiet glances. The aching realization that I was a stranger in a place that once knew me. I didn't cry. I didn't ask why it all felt so fragmented. I didn't try to solve the riddle of identity that hung in the air like incense smoke.

Because this…this was where I came from. And no matter how far I had run, no matter how polished my English or how many degrees I collected, this part of me would never really leave.

And I was learning not to push it away.

18: A Quiet Goodbye

On my final morning in the village, I woke up before my family and the rest of the villagers had risen. The humidity had not lifted, but there was a stillness in the air, like the earth was holding its breath. I put on the lightest clothes I had, tied my hair back, and walked alone toward the edge of the rice fields. The sun had not yet risen, and the world was still shrouded in darkness. The soft glow from the fireflies and lightning bugs created a rhythmic, almost melodic light, guiding me through the rice fields.

I carried with me a letter I had written the night before. Just a few pages scribbled on cheap notebook paper. It wasn't addressed to anyone specifically—just the past. In it, I wrote down everything I had never said out loud. To my younger self. To the adults who failed me. To the silence that used to scream so loud it hurt. I poured every ounce of hurt, of confusion, of grief into those pages. Then I folded it, one crease at a time, until it fit into the palm of my hand.

At the edge of the field, there was a small stream. The water moved lazily, warm, and brown with the dust of life. I knelt down, and without ceremony, I set the letter into the water. It didn't sink right away. It floated, bobbing gently, as if saying goodbye. Then, slowly, the paper took on water and drifted down, disappearing into the murk. I watched it until I couldn't see it anymore. And that was it.

No fireworks. No sudden feeling of freedom or rebirth. Just... quiet. But in that quiet, I felt a small shift. Like something heavy had moved a few inches off my chest. It was enough. Enough to stand up, brush the dirt off my knees, and walk back to the house.

It wasn't a grand ceremony. No one will write about it in a book of healing practices. But it was mine. My ritual. A small act of letting go. And in that act, I claimed something back for myself: my power, my peace, my choice to move forward without dragging all the broken pieces with me.

As cliché as it sounds, the idea came to me from the movie *The Shawshank Redemption*— specifically, the scene where a note is hidden in the wall. There weren't many similarities between the film and what I ended up doing...writing down my thoughts and letting them float away down a stream—but that morning, for some reason, that scene came to mind.

Unlike the movie, I didn't want my note to be found. It held emotions I wasn't ready for anyone else to read. Ironically, I laugh thinking about it now—my family doesn't understand English, and I doubt many people in the village would have either. I probably could have left it somewhere and no one would've known what it said.

**

I skipped breakfast that morning—I wasn't hungry, knowing I'd be returning to America later that day. The sun had barely begun to rise when the bus pulled up in front of my cousin's house. The air was thick and already humid, as it always is in the countryside of Vietnam.

I stepped out with a quiet heaviness, knowing this was it. This visit—the reunion—was coming to an end. My grandmother, 99 years old, almost completely blind, stood near the edge of the road. She couldn't see me, not really. But somehow, she knew. As I climbed onto the bus, she began to move toward me, her steps unsteady but determined. She called my name, and though I couldn't hear her clearly, I felt it. I felt her love, her desperation, her goodbye.

Then she did something I never expected—she chased after the bus.

That image is burned into me. My grandmother, frail and aged by nearly a century of hard living, running after me with more strength than I had ever seen. Her body, hunched from nearly a century of hard living, somehow found the strength to run after the bus as it pulled away. Her thin legs moved faster than I had ever seen, arms outstretched, as if she could reach through the distance and stop time itself.

In that moment, it wasn't about the past or the pain—it was something deeper, something universally human. A connection that anyone, regardless of history, could feel. And in the face of that, the sadness overwhelmed everything else. I pressed my face against the window, tears falling freely.

**

No one on the bus said a word. My sister sat beside me, quiet and still, and behind us were cousins and neighbors who were part of my forgotten beginnings. We rode together, a strange full circle, yet I felt like a stranger still.

I cried silently the entire way to the airport. Not loudly. Not visibly. But inwardly, with a pain that had waited 30 years to surface. I was crying for the grandmother I barely got to know. For the sister I found too late. For the life I might have had. I cried for the poverty and the beauty, the loss, and the love.

And yet, even through the ache, I carried something back with me—closure.

That trip didn't answer every question. It didn't erase the years of abandonment or the trauma that shaped me. But it gave me something I had never had before: the ability to shut doors I'd been standing in front of my entire life. I saw the faces behind the memories. I walked the dirt roads I once cried on. And in doing so, I found peace—not perfect peace, but a kind I could live with.

I was returning with it stitched into my story; softened, acknowledged, and finally, finally laid to rest.

**

When I got to the airport, I moved like a ghost through security and customs. People bustled around me, pulling suitcases, wrangling children, ordering coffee, arguing over gates and connections, but I was somewhere else entirely. Somewhere between two worlds, not fully in either one. I carried with me more than just my luggage. I carried names I had just learned, stories that had finally been told, and a version of myself I had been chasing across decades and continents.

As I sat by the window, waiting to board my flight, I leaned my forehead against the glass, letting it anchor me as the weight of the moment settled in. Outside, the sky had turned a soft, pale gray…muted and heavy, like the calm before a storm. The clouds hung low, thick with the promise of rain, as if Vietnam itself was holding back tears. It felt fitting, almost poetic…

I snapped a photo of the dull, gray sky and sent it to a friend with a half-joking caption: "Boo hoo, headed back to the States." It was my way of masking the bittersweet feeling with humor. Beneath the sarcasm, though, was a quiet heaviness. Leaving wasn't just about changing locations; it felt like closing a chapter I wasn't entirely ready to end.

I thought of my grandmother again; of her thin arms outstretched, how her voice carried so much weight while running after the bus. I thought of how many years we had lost. Of how many stories I never got to hear. There was so much left unsaid between us, so many questions I had only just begun to ask. And now, as I sat at the edge of departure, I felt the weight of it all—of time we could never reclaim, of words I'd never hear, of love that arrived too late.

**

Time—

To me, time is the invisible thread that binds everything together…past, present, and future. It's the quiet witness to all our joys and regrets, our beginnings, and endings. Time doesn't wait, but it remembers. It leaves traces in our memories, in the faces of those we love, and in the stories we tell when everything else is gone.

**

When my boarding group was called, I didn't want to stand. My legs felt heavy, like they knew that once I stepped onto that plane, something would change again. I wasn't the same person who had arrived. And I wasn't quite sure who I was returning as. But I got up anyway. I had made peace with not having all the answers.

Deep down, I wasn't sure if coming back to the States would make anything better. The thought of returning to my "real life" filled me with dread. Yes, I had found a sense of closure with my family in Vietnam—pieces of myself I had long buried were finally unearthed. But the wounds I carried back home hadn't magically healed. My friends were still gone. My dog, my companion through everything, was still gone. That pain didn't disappear just because I had rediscovered my roots.

I knew this trip wasn't a cure-all. It was a chapter closed, not the whole story rewritten. While one past was laid to rest, another storm still raged inside me. Grief, depression, and the quiet ache of loneliness were waiting for me like shadows at the door. I wasn't naïve about it. Healing is never linear.

**

The journey home was quiet. I slept in small, broken stretches, my dreams scattered and strange. When I landed, everything felt both familiar and foreign. The language, the air, the rhythm of things. I was back in the life I had built. My job. My routines. But something had shifted in me.

I came back to a dog who wagged his tail like nothing had changed. He was happy, eager, full of love—like he'd been waiting his whole life just for me to walk through that door. But while he welcomed me home, so did the darkness. It was still there, lurking in the corners, wrapping itself around me like an old familiar coat. The depression didn't end with the trip. It didn't vanish just because I had boarded a plane, cried in front of my grandmother, or touched the soil of where I came from.

In the weeks that followed, I found myself slowing down. Sitting in the quiet more often. Writing without censoring myself. Letting the grief wash over me in waves instead of trying to dam it up with productivity or distraction. Something inside me had shifted. I had learned, slowly, how to sit in silence—not the kind that suffocates you, but the kind that teaches you to breathe. To sit with yourself. To not run. That trip didn't cure me, but it cracked open a piece of the wall I'd built around myself. It gave me something I hadn't had in a long time: clarity. Not happiness. Not peace. But clarity.

And from clarity came closure—not all of it, but some. It was one piece of the puzzle. One part of the healing. It would take me another two years to crawl out of the fog, to truly find my footing again. But at least, this time, I had somewhere to start.

19: This Version of Me

The café is quiet now, the kind of quiet that settles in between the lunch and dinner rush. The espresso machine no longer hisses, and the low hum of conversation begins to taper off. I look up from my laptop, eyes tired.

And then I see her—a familiar face. A friend I've grown close to since moving here. She walks in like she always does, with that calm confidence that makes people want to lean in and stay awhile. When she spots me by the window, her smile stretches wide and warm, and she makes her way over.

"Hey, mind if I join you?" she asks, dropping her bag beside the chair before I even answer.

"Of course," I say, and I feel a bit of weight lift from my shoulders.

She's from South Africa and every time I hear her accent, it brings a smile to my face. Her cheerful, carefree attitude is simply contagious, and it always draws me in.

We talk. She tells me about her day—teaching, errands, a funny story from the street. I tell her about mine, a day filled with coffee, false starts, and the stubborn blinking of a blank page. Eventually, I tell her what I'm working on.

"I'm writing a book," I admit.

Her eyebrows raise, curious. "Really? What kind?"

I hesitate. She doesn't know my story. Not that I'm adopted. Not about the trauma. Not about the journey that brought me here. "It's kind of a memoir," I say. "It's messy. But it's helping me heal."

She doesn't pry. She just nods and shares more about her own life—her siblings, growing up in South Africa, the boy who broke her heart in college. We laugh, exchange soft glances during quiet pauses, and feel the kind of ease that only comes when someone sees you, even if they don't know everything yet.

After an hour, she checks the time.

"I should get going," she says as she stands. "Let's catch up again soon?"

"Definitely," I say, and I mean it.

Once she leaves, I glance at the time. 6:00 p.m. Another full day at the café. I laugh under my breath…what must the staff think of me? The girl who parks herself here from 7 a.m. to closing. The one who types, deletes, sighs, and stares into space for hours. The one who orders coffee but barely drinks it.

Maybe today they're surprised. Today, I actually write.

I close my laptop, nod to the waitress who's seen this struggle unfold in slow motion day after day, and head out into the evening air.

**

I've been too intimidated to ride a motorbike in Ho Chi Minh City. The traffic here is nothing short of chaotic—it's the best way I can describe it. So, instead, I've been relying on Grab, which is basically the same as Uber back in the States.

I open the app, choose my ride, and just as I am ready to click "submit" to find a driver. I cancel and decide to walk home instead.

What's amusing about walking in Vietnam, though, is that people can instantly tell if you're a local or a foreigner. Locals rarely walk outside, not just out of preference but because they're often wary of the sun, which can be harsh on the skin. Foreigners, especially Westerners, though, seem to almost worship the sun, embracing its warmth as part of the experience. Even though the sun has long set by 6 p.m., locals here still seem to believe that the sun might suddenly reappear, as though it's just waiting to catch them.

**

When I finally step through the front gate, the last blush of sunset fading behind the buildings, I already know who's waiting for me.

Before I even unlock the door, I hear the soft scratching from the other side…little frantic taps like Morse code: *Where have you been? I missed you. Come home already.*

As soon as I open the door, there he is. My three-legged shadow, Petey. Tail wagging so hard it sends his whole body into a wobble. That lopsided, toothy grin only rescue dogs have—the one that says they remember, even if they can't say it.

He bounces around me like I've been gone for a lifetime, even though it's just been a day. I drop my backpack, crouch down, and let him cover me in kisses. I bury my face in his neck. He smells like warm sun and the tiniest bit of dirt—proof of his latest adventure with his dog walker who stops by once a day to let him out.

"I missed you too, bubba," I whisper.

There's something sacred about this moment, every time. He doesn't know the things I've done. He doesn't care that I've made mistakes. That I spent years and am still trying to find myself, that I sometimes cry alone at night, or that I can't always finish what I start.

He just knows I came back.

We settle into our little rhythm—he eats while I toss off my shoes. I fix myself a bowl of something quick, toast and eggs, and we curl up on the carpet together afterward. Not the couch. Not the bed. Just the floor. It feels more honest. Like I'm grounding myself again.

He rests his head on my legs and looks up at me with the same wide-eyed joy as a dog seeing their person for the first time… even though I've already been home for an hour. His excitement doesn't fade; it's unwavering. His tail keeps wagging nonstop. Even at six years old, he still acts like a puppy, full of energy and pure, loyal love.

This is the part of the day where I exhale. Where the silence is no longer deafening but comforting. Where I no longer feel alone, even though it's just the two of us.

Petey is not just a dog. He's been my emotional anchor. My co-pilot in this thing I call life. A witness to my daily highs and lows, but always there. No questions. No judgments. Just wagging, waiting, and loving.

He has been by my side through the dark years of 2022 to 2024. He was with me in 2019 when I lost a dear friend, again in 2021 when another close friend passed away, and in 2022 when his sister—my beloved dog of 18 years—died. In just six years of life, he's endured more dark hours than bright days. And yet, what makes him so incredibly special to me isn't just what he's been through—it's how he continues to live. Every single day, he wakes up with joy in his heart, wagging his tail with a kind of optimism that's contagious. Even on three legs, he moves forward without hesitation, as if the past has no hold on him. His spirit is nothing short of admirable. He reminds me, without saying a word, what resilience really looks like.

And as I sit there, stroking the soft velvet fur behind his ear, I think back to this morning. That blinking cursor. The self-doubt. The wondering if I would ever get it done.

But I did something today.

I wrote.

I started.

And I came home—not just to this apartment, but to this version of myself that I've been trying to love more fully.

Despite everything, I'm here.

And so is Petey.

And I smile.

Because today, I did something I didn't think I could. I write. I start. And that's everything. Today, just sitting down and writing, I feel alive again. It's a rare, fleeting sense of peace; like I've pressed pause on the chaos inside my mind. It's not everything, but it's something. And today, I feel proud of myself for starting. For doing the hard thing.

Despite the mess. Despite the mistakes. Despite all the idiotic choices, the heartbreaks, the spirals—I am proud of myself.

**

My friends and family often ask me how long I intend to stay in Vietnam. I don't know how long I'll be here in Vietnam. Maybe a few more months. Maybe longer. Maybe less. There's no real plan, just a quiet decision to take each day as it comes and to make the best of what I have while I'm here.

My phone buzzes softly beside my coffee cup. It's a message from my sister.

"Chủ nhật này em làm gì?"
What are you doing this Sunday?

I type back without even thinking:
"Same thing as always."

A few seconds later, her reply comes through.
"Okay, I'll see you at 10am."

Every Sunday since I landed in Saigon, we've made it a ritual when I am in town—dog walking at a local dog shelter. It started as something small, something I could offer her. A way to fill our time, to share an activity that didn't require language or explanations. Now, it's become our thing.

We walk side by side, sometimes quietly, other times laughing as the dogs pull us along tangled sidewalks. We speak in fragments. Google Translate filling the space between our broken phrases. It's clumsy, imperfect, but it's ours.

My sister—like many people in Vietnam—grew up without much education or awareness about animals, especially dogs. To be honest, animal welfare has never been a cultural priority in a country that has endured decades of war and poverty. The impact of that kind of history runs deep. When you've been surrounded by survival, compassion toward animals often takes a back seat. In some areas, dogs and cats are still viewed primarily as food or property, not companions.

That mindset isn't easy to unlearn, especially when it's all you've ever known. But what I admire about my sister is her willingness to learn. She's been open to understanding who I am and why I love dogs so deeply. She's asked questions, listened to my stories, and even tried to engage with the animals I've brought around. That effort—small as it may seem—is monumental in a context like ours.

It means something to me. It means she's trying to bridge a gap between our worlds. It means she sees me. And for that, I'm proud of her. Because love isn't always shown in the ways we expect—it's sometimes in the quiet willingness to learn something unfamiliar, just to make someone you care about feel understood.

**

I try to do as much as I can with my sister while I'm here. Not because I have to, but because I want to. Maybe it's guilt. Maybe it's love. Probably both. We've gone to Hanoi together. Halong

Bay. Mui Ne. Amusement parks where we laughed until we cried on the rides. New restaurants with food she's never tried. We sit across from each other, sometimes not saying much at all, but just being.

Every place we've visited has been a first for her. While I'm here in Vietnam, I'm doing my best to introduce her to as much as I can—to let her fully experience the richness and beauty of the country she grew up in. I want her to see it through fresh eyes, to feel the warmth, the culture, and the vibrant life that makes this place so special.

I'm still learning Vietnamese, but I can't say much beyond a handful of words. Everything is still mostly gestures, laughs, and Google Translate screens. But we make it work. Connection…I'm learning, doesn't always need full sentences. Sometimes presence is enough.

She's quiet, soft-spoken, always observing. I don't know how she feels about me—about all of this. But I hope, deep down, that she's proud of me. I hope the times we've had means something to her, even if she never says it. I hope she has some kind of closure too. Because I know I've needed it more than I ever admitted.

And while I do plan to go back to the U.S., I still don't know exactly when. But until then, I'm here. I'm trying. Trying to be present, to be whole, to show up for my sister in all the small ways I can. Because we lost so much time, and I can't get that back. But what I can do is show up now, as best as I can—with the time I've been given.

That's all I have to offer. And maybe that's enough.

20: The Story I Needed to Tell

When I first arrived in Vietnam, I came with a heart half-shut. I told myself I was coming here to work, to build my business, to find peace.

Ha…let's just say my first few weeks were a complete disaster, and everything that could go wrong, did.

When I first arrived in Vietnam, everything felt like chaos. Nothing was going right. I had the hardest time adjusting—culturally, emotionally, mentally. Just days in, my credit card was hacked, and I was completely stuck, relying on my parents to send me a new one from overseas. This card did not get to me until two months later.

The challenge with Vietnam is that none of the major U.S. banks operate here, which made accessing cash incredibly difficult. With Vietnam's strict banking regulations, withdrawing money from local banks was nearly impossible unless I opened a Vietnamese bank account. But even that wasn't simple—it required a temporary residence card, which I could only obtain through legal employment with a recognized company in Vietnam. It was a complicated, frustrating process, and the first few months felt like a blur of financial stress and red tape.

I remember sitting on the floor of my apartment, feeling like I had hit rock bottom. I asked myself—over and over again—why am I even here? What was I thinking? I missed my friends. I missed my family. I missed the familiar rhythm of life back in the States.

I didn't know how to explain what I was feeling to anyone around me, so I did what I've always done when emotions get too big to say out loud: I wrote. My laptop became my safe space, my private journal where I could pour everything out—confusion, sadness, frustration, longing. It was the only place where the noise of my mind found clarity.

Then one afternoon, the internet in my apartment went out. I was told it could be hours, maybe longer, because of street construction. Restless and needing to write, I wandered to a coffee shop just down the road. It was small, tucked between a pharmacy and a clothing shop, but warm and quiet. I opened my laptop, intending to journal, but something shifted in me that day. I didn't just write for myself. I started writing for the version of me who needed to hear these words. That's when the idea of this memoir began.

**

I chose to write this memoir as a way to rediscover who I am. To make sense of the pieces of my past, my identity, and everything I've carried with me but never fully understood. In the midst of uncertainty, loneliness, and change, writing became a way to reflect, to heal, and to reconnect with the version of myself I had long buried beneath survival, obligation, and silence. This memoir isn't just a collection of memories—it's a journey inward, a quiet but determined search for clarity, purpose, and belonging.

And while I may not have found all the answers, I found pieces of myself I didn't know were still out there—buried under decades of silence, adoption papers, and unspoken grief.

I found my sister. I found my grandmother.
I found a past that hurt, yes—but also healed.

**

The days have softened here in Vietnam. The rainy season has come and gone, leaving behind skies I've learned to read like the lines of a familiar poem.

And yet, on certain days, the rain finds its way back. I no longer flinch when the clouds gather. Somehow, I always know it's nearby. Now, when the rain begins to fall, I welcome it. I let the soft percussion of water tapping against the windows become the soundtrack to my afternoons. It soothes more than it interrupts. There's a quiet beauty in letting life unfold without resistance. Somewhere between the tangled streets of Saigon and the slow drip of Vietnamese coffee, I've found a rhythm.

**

It's still not perfect. Some days, I wake up and it's just there again—sadness, confusion, guilt—all tangled up and sitting in my chest, and I still have moments where I question everything. But this rhythm? It's real. It's mine. And for the first time in a long time, that feels like enough.

I spend my days trying to adjust, meeting people, setting up the business, figuring out how to navigate the streets without getting lost (which happens often). The food is incredible. Street vendors selling pho, bánh mì, and fresh fruit shakes at every corner. I've never felt so full and yet so far away from anything I've ever known.

In the evenings, I sit by the window, watching the sun lower behind the skyline of Saigon, its last light casting a golden hue across the balcony outside my apartment. The motorbikes hum like a chorus, the street vendors shout with rhythm, and neon signs flicker to life one by one. The noise, the people, the endless energy—it's chaotic—yet strangely comforting. Some nights, it pulses through me like electricity, like proof that I'm still here, still breathing, still part of something. And on those nights, it's enough to make me feel alive again.

Other nights, it's quieter. Not outside, but inside me. I sit alone in that same spot, tea cooling in my hands, eyes tracing the same skyline I've seen for months, and I wonder—what am I doing here? What am I really chasing?

**

For so long, I believed I was running from my past, from pain, from the version of myself I didn't know how to love. But maybe, for the first time, I'm not running away. Maybe I'm running toward something. Something bigger than me. Maybe this book—this messy, vulnerable, unfinished story—is my calling. Maybe it's the very thing I needed to write, not just to make sense of my life, but to reach someone else who feels just as lost.

Maybe it's meant for another girl sitting in a coffee shop halfway around the world, wondering if she matters. Wondering if her story is worth telling. If her life, with all its broken pieces and hard edges, can still be beautiful.

Because that's the thing—I've learned that life isn't always about clarity or perfection. It's about the moments. The small ones that sneak up on you in between heartbreak and healing. It's the quiet joy of walking your dog at dusk, the ache in your chest when someone remembers your name, the relief in crying without shame. The grief, the gratitude. The laughter through tears. The not knowing, and still choosing to keep going.

And that's where the beauty lives—in the in-between. In the fact that even after everything, there is still hope. Still love. Still light.

**

It's strange to feel this calm after a life of running. Running from my past. From shame. From unanswered questions. From the broken parts of myself I didn't think I could ever face. But something about sitting with my grief in a foreign land—something about walking dogs with my sister, sipping cà phê sữa đá alone in a crowded café, or simply letting myself be angry, sad, and joyful without judgment—has allowed me to finally catch my breath.

And in catching my breath, I found something else: peace. For the first time in my life, I am not just surviving. I'm living.

It's not the kind of peace most people imagine. Not a serene, picture-perfect calm or the absence of noise. It's deeper than that. It's a peace where I no longer wake up with a tight chest or battle those sudden waves of panic that used to crash over me. It's the absence of that constant, nagging voice in my head telling me I'm not enough, that I'm falling behind.

Instead, I've found a sense of ease where I'm no longer obsessed with what's next or haunted by what's already happened. I simply exist in the moment. I enjoy what's in front of me. I feel grounded. I feel present. I feel content.

This peace I've found isn't about everything being perfect; it's about finally understanding what it means to live the journey, not chase the finish line. Like the saying goes, *life is about the journey, not the destination.* And for the first time in a long time, I'm not rushing toward something. I'm walking, slowly, intentionally, and fully here for the journey itself.

**

I'm no longer running from my story. I've lived it. I've written it. And somehow, in stringing together each painful, beautiful, messy chapter, I've come back to myself.

And that's the difference now.

Before, I was always looking for a way to outrun the pain. I kept my past hidden, tucked away in the corners of my mind like old photo albums I couldn't bear to open. But healing doesn't come from forgetting. It comes from remembering and giving those memories a new ending.

That's what this book is.

A new ending.

Not to erase what was done, but to tell it with my own voice. To take back the story and tell it honestly—messy, complicated, beautiful, flawed. A story of an adoptee. A sister. A daughter. A woman still learning how to forgive, how to stay soft in a world that tried to harden her. A woman who cries easily now and no longer hides it. A woman who laughs more freely, trusts her heart more deeply, and lets go more gently.

**

There's a message waiting for me on my phone when I get home this evening. It's from my cousin—one of the few who I've stayed in touch with after I visited in 2022.
"Grandmother is asking about you again."

I smile. My grandmother, now 102, still remembers the sound of my voice. She may not see or hear anymore, but somehow, she knows when it is me walking into the room. The last time I visited, she traced the lines of my face with her hands like she was reading a map of time and memory. I think she saw me in a way no one else ever has.

I message back:
"Tell her I'll be there in two weeks."

It's time to go back to Song Vân. Not to stay, not to start over—but to return, simply as I am. Not the abandoned child. Not the angry teenager. Not the perfectionist woman trying to outpace her own sadness. Just me: Tia. Someone who's learning to be okay with not having it all figured out.

**

I glance down at my phone—another notification. This time, it's a message from my mom: *"Call me."*

It's simple, no emojis, no punctuation. Just those two words.

I open Facebook Messenger and tap the call button. It's the only way we talk now. She doesn't know how to call me, but I've learned how to reach her across oceans and time zones through this one app. It doesn't cost anything to call internationally with it. The screen rings a few times before her face pops up, a little pixelated, but familiar. Comforting.

"Hi, Mom," I say.

She smiles, a little surprised each time I call, like she wasn't expecting me to actually do it. Her voice crackles a bit through the connection, but I can hear the warmth in it.

We chat. I tell her I'll be going to the countryside in two weeks to visit bà. I can already see her smile softening when I mention my grandmother's name. I update her on my life here in Saigon—how the rainy seasons passed, how I'm still working on my book from cafés, how I've made a routine that somehow feels like mine now.

She listens quietly, nodding, her face glowing in the low light of her kitchen back home. Then she says simply, "Have fun. Love you."

That's always her way…short sentences, big meaning. It's her way of letting me go while still holding me close.

The call ends and it hits me how, no matter how grown you are, a mother's words never really change. The same gentle reminders, the same warmth—just like when you were little.

**

I glance over at Petey, stretched out on the floor, belly full and completely at peace. He's always like this—content, easygoing, almost too perfect. Like happiness just comes naturally to him. He doesn't care how much I've accomplished today. He doesn't know I finally broke through my writer's block. He only knows I'm here. And that's all that matters to him.

We curl up together on the floor, his large but comforting and familiar body pressed up to mine, I breathe deep and exhale all the weight I used to carry alone. I breathe in the quiet joy of being still. No flights to catch. No deadlines to chase. Just this moment.

Tomorrow will come, and with it, new choices, new chapters. But tonight, for the first time in a long time, I feel light.

**

In two weeks, I'll sit beside my grandmother again. Maybe we'll share a quiet moment. But these days, she sleeps more than she's awake. And truthfully, I might just be sitting quietly beside her while she rests, listening to her breath.

She might not even know I'm there.

But I'll be there anyway.

And while I don't always feel a deep emotional connection when I'm with my grandmother, I've come to understand that presence itself can be a form of love. In these final years of her life, the most meaningful thing I can offer is simply being there—showing up, sitting beside her, and letting her know she's not alone. And if my presence brings even the faintest flicker of comfort or recognition, then it will be enough.

Even if she forgets I came, I'll remember.

And I'll know that I did what mattered most—I came back.

**

If you ask me if I'm healed—especially after writing through all these chapters, reliving memories that were more sad than joyful—the truth is, no. I'm not healed. Not in the way people hope healing looks. Not in the way that wraps everything up with a neat bow.

Writing this book didn't erase the pain. It didn't undo the loneliness of my childhood or the ache of all the years I spent feeling like I didn't belong. If anything, it brought those moments back into the light—sharper, more vivid, more real than I'd allowed myself to feel in a long time.

But maybe that's what healing actually looks like—not erasing the pain but making space for it. Naming it. Facing it. And then choosing, every day, to live anyway. To love anyway. To keep going.

And maybe that's more than enough.

Because healing isn't a destination—it's a choice I make every day. To wake up and try again. To keep my heart open even when it aches. To forgive parts of myself I once thought were unlovable. To choose softness when the world taught me to harden. To speak even when my voice trembles.

This isn't the end—it's the beginning of something new.

A new chapter where I no longer carry shame like armor. Where I no longer need to prove my worth to feel worthy. Where I make peace with the girl I used to be—the one who laid still at night in the orphanage, feeling invisible, unwanted, unloved. I carry her with me now, not as a shadow, but as a survivor. She is the reason I can sit here, writing this. She is the reason I keep going.

If she could see me now, I think she'd be proud—not because I've figured it all out, but because I never stopped trying.

**

I often find myself thinking about that little girl in the orphanage—the one who laid so still at night, angry at the world, too tired to cry, too guarded to hope. I wonder what she would think if she could see me now.

Would she recognize this version of us? The woman sitting in a sunlit café, writing her story out loud instead of hiding it away? The one who lets herself cry, laugh, love…even after everything?

Sometimes I imagine her peeking into my life now, skeptical at first. Maybe she'd cross her arms and ask, "What took you so long?" Or maybe she wouldn't say anything at all—just watch, wide-eyed, as if trying to make sense of how we made it from there to here.

I think she'd be proud, in her own quiet way. Not because everything is perfect. Not because the pain is gone. But because I didn't let it break me. Because I kept going. Because I came back— not just to the country where she was born— but to her.

And in doing so, I didn't just find a part of myself—I found her again.

We're no longer just surviving. We're living. For her. With her. As her.

And maybe this is the truest form of healing.

**

And that's what I leave you with. Not a perfect ending. Not a neatly tied-up story. But a real one.

One with cracked edges and open hands. One that honors every loss, every joy, every silence and scream. One that says: You are allowed to grow, to grieve, to glow all at once.

So no, this isn't the end.

It's the beginning of living more truthfully, loving more freely, and finally, enjoying the journey.

Here I am.
Still healing.
Still writing.
Still becoming.

And maybe that's where all our stories truly begin.

The first picture my parents saw of me.

With the director of the Orphanage.

The day I was adopted. I am in the red jacket.

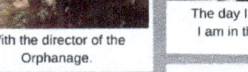

The fields I used to run and hide in

My biological sister and I

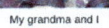

My grandma and I

Childhood house

My childhood in America. Left to right: my friend, myself, my sister (adopted).

Sealing my adoption at a courthouse in the US. Left to right: my father, grandmother, myself, my sister, and grandfather (far right)

Celebrating the day my adoption was official in the US. Left to right: my grandfather, dad, myself, mom

132

The coffeeshop where this book was written.

About the Author

Tia Heard is a writer, traveler, and fierce advocate for the overlooked, both people and animals alike. Born in Vietnam and raised in the United States, Tia brings a unique, cross-cultural lens to her storytelling, writing from a place of raw honesty, compassion, and lived experience.

She is the proud dog mom of two rescues: one three-legged dog adopted in the U.S., and another found on the streets of Vietnam. Her love for animals mirrors her deeper passion for helping the marginalized and voiceless in society. Whether she's volunteering with orphaned children, or advocating for animal welfare, Tia is driven by a deep desire to give back.

Tia is also a small business owner, having launched her own venture with the goal of inspiring and empowering others to pursue their own paths, even when those paths are messy and uncertain. Whether through storytelling, teaching, or entrepreneurship, she believes in the power of showing up, being vulnerable, and creating meaning from life's most difficult chapters.

A firm believer in healing through expression, *My Name Is Almost* is her first book. A deeply personal memoir that speaks to survival, identity, and love in all its messy, imperfect forms. Tia continues to write, explore the world, and create spaces of hope wherever she lands.